GETTING ST

TEACHER
CLARITY

GETTING STARTED WITH

TEACHER CLARITY

Ready-to-use research-based strategies to develop learning intentions, foster student autonomy, and engage students

Marine Freibrun

Published in the United States by:
Ulysses Press
PO Box 3440
Berkeley, CA 94703
www.ulyssespress.com

ISBN: 978-1-64604-134-3
Library of Congress Control Number: 2020946973

Printed in the United States by Kingery Printing Company
10 9 8 7 6 5 4 3 2 1

Acquisitions editor: Claire Sielaff
Managing editor: Claire Chun
Editor: Renee Rutledge
Proofreader: Barbara Schultz
Front cover design: Justin Shirley
Cover art: © Aleksandr Bryliaev/shutterstock.com
Interior design and layout: what!design @ whatweb.com
Interior photos: Marine Freibrun

CONTENTS

CHAPTER 1

WHAT IS TEACHER CLARITY?

My experience as a student in school was largely made up of listening to teachers regurgitate information from a textbook, doing the work because I was told to do it, and getting a letter grade that didn't really reflect any progression of my learning. Not to mention the anxiety and stress of not understanding every topic, lesson, or skill that I was being taught while also being afraid to ask for help. Now, to be fair, I did occasionally have some amazing teachers who went above and beyond to support me and my learning journey.

Here's what I remember most about those teachers and their classrooms:

1. I knew why we were learning what we were learning.

2. I felt cared for and valued, and I was never afraid to ask for help.

3. I knew those teachers believed in me and that they knew I would eventually "get it."

Ultimately, those teachers communicated expectations, created an environment of trust, and believed learning was a progression. I strive to bring the same values to my students.

Part of doing that is asking myself an essential question each and every time I am planning out my week: How can I effectively communicate the ultimate goal of learning and engage my students in the learning process in order to help them succeed?

Teacher clarity is the process that helped me answer that question.

SO, WHAT IS TEACHER CLARITY?

Teacher clarity is not just another thing to do. It's not another gimmick. It's a culture of teaching and collaboration. Actually, it's a mindset, one that is essential in supporting students. Teacher clarity ultimately makes teaching a lot more streamlined and purposeful; therefore, it cuts out the nonessential things we don't need to teach.

This can be a complex process and might seem daunting to take on along with the numerous other requirements of managing a classroom. That's why, in this book, we'll take things step-by-step and break down each factor that goes into teacher clarity.

"Clarity" means the quality of being coherent and intelligible. In my teaching experience, I've felt that I've shown students clarity in my lesson design and learning intentions. But the truth is, the only person who understood things clearly during the school day was me—the classroom teacher. My students were compliant, but compliance doesn't equate to learning. What I lacked was genuine clarity.

Teacher clarity takes limits off student learning by shifting the teaching mindset to plan lessons and units intentionally. As explained by Professor John Hattie in *10 Mindframes for Visible Learning: Teaching for Success* (2017), teacher clarity helps teachers understand what we need to teach, how to teach it, and how we'll measure our students' success.

Let's look more closely at what that means.

WHAT WE NEED TO TEACH

In order to truly understand what we need to teach, we need to look closely at what the standards (whether they're Common Core State Standards or a state's specific standards) are asking of our students. We can do this by deconstructing the standard and identifying the essential skills needed to meet that standard. This involves not only carefully planning a lesson but also creating and setting learning intentions.

Learning intentions are what teachers want students to learn, and these need to be clear to both the students and the teachers. If we have a better understanding of what we need to teach in a lesson, unit, or activity, then we're more capable of articulating that information to our students. If students know what success looks like and what steps they need to take to get there, then they will be much more successful, and they can also meet and exceed standards with much more support. We'll cover this in Chapter 4.

HOW TO TEACH IT

By identifying *what* we need to teach, we gain a better understanding of *how* to teach it. When you think of how to teach material, lesson planning and design probably come to mind. Although both are extremely important, more layers need to be added. When it comes to teaching standards, we also have to think about how we're grouping specific standards together, what we want our students to achieve by the end of learning a group of standards, and how to plan with the end in mind to communicate the final learning goal to our students. We'll do this together in Chapter 5.

HOW WE MEASURE STUDENT SUCCESS

When we measure student success we look at where students are in the learning process. We don't only look at a unit test or assessment they have finished. Think of student success as progress, not perfection. Through teacher clarity, students can also assess their own progress through **success criteria**, "the specific, concrete, measurable statements that describe what success looks like when the learning goal is reached" (Hattie et al. 2017, 39).

For example, if you're working with your students on an opinion writing piece, a success criterion might look like a target response that students can refer to along with a rubric to help them meet the criteria for that writing piece. Teachers and students would work in a partnership, communicating about the students' progress toward meeting a specific learning intention. We'll look at this further in Chapter 8.

Teacher clarity supports your teaching efforts because it allows you to be more aware of and engaged with the effect you have on your students. Ultimately, teacher clarity amounts to how clearly teachers and students communicate with one another to explain their level of understanding of a learning intention, activity, or goal (Hattie et al. 2017, 38).

According to *The Teacher Clarity Playbook*, teacher clarity should be emphasized across four areas (Hattie et al. 2018, xiv). Having teacher clarity across these four areas involves a lot of collaboration and planning, as well as communication between the students and the teacher:

1. **Clarity of organization.** Through clarity of organization, lessons and assignments are linked back to learning objectives and intentions.

2. **Clarity of explanation.** When information is explained to students, is relevant and accurate, and students can clearly understand what is expected of them during a lesson or activity.

3. **Clarity of examples and guided practice.** Students are given the opportunity to work gradually toward independence through a gradual release model. Students make progress as they're able to work with less and less teacher support.

4. **Clarity of assessment.** Through teacher clarity, teachers actively seek feedback from students through assessments (informal, formative, summative, self) to gauge the next steps in the learning progression.

Teacher clarity helps teachers understand and remember the importance of our role in our students' lives. "Know thy impact," as John Hattie says (Hattie et al. 2012, ix).

HOW TO BEGIN

So, how do you start being more intentional about promoting teacher clarity with your students or on your grade-level team?

START SMALL

When you start thinking about all that goes into teacher clarity (assessments, planning, explicit instruction, success criteria, target responses, etc.) it may feel a little overwhelming. Starting with something manageable can help lessen the stress as well as help you integrate teacher clarity more seamlessly into your daily teaching routine. With that said, think about starting in one place. Maybe you want to focus on assessment, or maybe you think starting with success criteria would be more feasible for your daily lessons. You can even start with one core subject and integrate a backward map of your unit, along with a target response. The point is, you don't have to implement everything at once in order to develop teacher clarity. If you start small you can build upon what you've started with and move forward with more stability and knowledge.

CREATE GOALS

Think about where you want to be in two to three months' time. Do you want to have a solid plan for formative assessments? Do you want to have your learning intentions and success criteria planned out for a math unit? Do you want to create target responses for a writing standard in your grade level? When you think about where you want to be in two to three months, you can then start backward planning your own path. Determine a goal, and then ask yourself, "What steps will I need to take in order to meet my goal?" Then take those steps to get there. Enlist the support of your grade-level team, your administrators, or your colleagues from other school sites. Show them what you're up to and develop goals together.

Here's a quick example:

> **Goal:** In two to three months' time, I'd like to have a series of formative assessments in the area of 5th-grade math standards about decimals. I would like to use these assessments to monitor my students' progress toward mastering each standard involving decimals.

My plan:

1. Determine the standards that I need to address with my students.

2. Group the standards based on difficulty and how closely they match up with each other. For example, can two to three standards easily be assessed on the same assessment?

3. Determine how many assessments I need to create in order to determine my students' progress and need for extension or support.

4. Plan out a time frame for the lessons and assessments.

If you start with one goal, one block of standards, or as a team, creating teacher clarity can become more manageable. You can take the same steps from other goals and easily incorporate them into your next goal. Just build upon what you're already doing.

YOU CAN'T
GET THERE ALONE

Teacher clarity requires a lot of work. But done correctly and collaboratively, this work benefits our students immensely. Imagine getting to the point of purposeful and intentional lesson planning and data analysis with your grade-level team. When you work together, great things happen for your kids, which is probably the reason you became a teacher. According to *Learning by Doing: A Handbook for Professional Learning Communities at Work*, the purpose of collaboration is to "help more students achieve at higher levels," and this can only happen if educators are engaged and focused on doing what's best for kids (DuFour et al. 2016, 59).

One way to collaborate with your grade-level team effectively, efficiently, and with intention is through a **professional learning community (PLC)**. In a PLC, teachers work collaboratively in an ongoing process to achieve better results for the students they serve.

The authors of *Learning by Doing* emphasize that whether or not you're engaging in PLCs at your school site, these four questions at the crux of PLCs are essential for creating teacher clarity among grade-level team members:

1. What do we want our students to know and be able to do?

2. How will we know if each student has learned it?

3. How will we respond when some students do not learn it?

4. How will we extend the learning for students who have demonstrated proficiency?

Through collaboration and the common goal of creating teacher clarity comes collective teacher efficacy, the belief of teachers in their ability to positively affect students. Collective teacher efficacy yields an effect size of 1.57 (Hattie et al. 2018). **Effect size** is the method for comparing results between two groups. It is valuable for quantifying the effectiveness of educational strategies and really determining the size of the effect. In turn this helps teachers have more knowledge about which strategies to use in comparison to others. In order to show an improvement in student learning, there must be an effect size of at least 0.40. The effect size of 0.40 is a year's growth in a year's time. The effect size for teacher clarity is 0.75—that's almost two years' growth in one year's time!

Imagine the difference that kind of impact can make on all our students.

YOU'VE GOT THIS!

Teaching with clarity can seem overwhelming. But you know what? You've got this! We're going to break everything down in the chapters ahead, and you're going to be ready to support your students with clarity, organization, and purpose. Now that you know the importance of teacher clarity, in the next chapter we'll go into how to develop a teacher clarity relationship with your students and how to support their self-awareness of what they're learning through communication and a solid partnership with you, their teacher.

Your students are so lucky to have a teacher who is preparing to better support them through teacher clarity.

Let's reflect...

What do you remember most about the teachers who have impacted you?

THREE IMPACTFUL MEMORIES FROM TEACHERS

How can those memories translate to help you promote teacher clarity in your classroom?

THREE SIMPLE THINGS I CAN DO TO START PROMOTING TEACHER CLARITY

CHAPTER 2

STUDENT AWARENESS AND PARTNERSHIP

At the center of teacher clarity is developing a strong relationship between students and teachers that values communication, respect, and a shared appreciation for monitoring progress toward meeting learning goals.

The most effective ways I have created this relationship with students in my classroom are:

- Communicating the learning intention at the start of each lesson

- Implementing the use of levels of understanding throughout each lesson

- Empowering my students to self-assess at the end of the lesson during independent practice

Let's break down these steps and look into this process further.

COMMUNICATING THE LEARNING INTENTION

Did you know that a child's attention span is approximately their age, in minutes?

Based on this calculation, as a 5th-grade teacher, I would estimate that my students' attention span would be anywhere from 9 to 11 minutes. That's why I intentionally plan brain breaks or stretch breaks every 10 minutes—so my students have an opportunity to refocus on any given task.

When I first started teaching, I spent a lot of my lesson time on a very long and unnecessary "anticipatory set." You know, the part of the lesson when you're supposed to get the kids really excited about what you're about to teach. The problem was that I spent so much time reading a long story, going into detail about an experience that would relate to the lesson, or playing a game to get my students engaged that by the time I was ready to share the learning intention, their attention spans had already been all used up!

I realized I was losing my students at the most crucial part of the lesson, when I share the learning intention. The learning intention states the goal of the lesson for the students, providing teacher clarity at the onset of the lesson. It is also an opportunity to engage students in a conversation about their level of understanding before the lesson continues. If students' attention is gone by the time you state the learning intention, chances are they're not engaged, ready to self-assess, or ready to hear what the remainder of the lesson is about, which can lead to confusion or a lack of comprehension during the lesson.

I knew I needed to make a change to help my students. I shifted my lesson design (which we'll dive into more deeply in Chapters

4 through 6) to make sure my students were alert and engaged when I stated the learning intention. This is not to say that I took away my fun and interesting anticipatory set; I just made sure to make it more succinct, intentional, and connected to the learning intention.

Here's how:

If my students' attention span is about 10 minutes on average, I make sure to state the lesson's learning intention and clearly model the new skill within that 10-minute time span. Modeling a new skill explicitly shows students how to complete a skill using metacognition and specific steps. Giving students the opportunity to see a skill clearly modeled supports teacher clarity while also providing the preparation and support they'll need to be successful in the gradual release, where students practice the skill with teacher support, and independent practice.

I also ensure that I engage my students in the lesson by connecting it to the learning intention.

Here's a sample of a 3rd-grade lesson I taught my students:

Standard: CCSS.ELA-LITERACY.RI.3.5: Use text features and search tools (e.g., key words, sidebars, hyperlinks) to locate information relevant to a given topic efficiently.

Learning intention: Learning how to use text features to locate specific information when reading a text.

Anticipatory set: To start the lesson with an **anticipatory set** (I also like to use the term "**hook**," because I am hooking my students into the lesson), share this picture of one of my favorite stores, Walmart.

Making a connection: Make a connection to the aisle signs in the photo and how they are similar to text features when you're reading informational text. I tell my students that I love shopping, and that whenever I visit a new store (or a new

Walmart), I use the aisle signs to help me identify where I can find the pens, white board markers, or other supplies I might need. The whole connection should take about two minutes to explain. Afterward, state the learning intention.

Learning Intention

We are learning how to use text features to locate specific information when reading informational text.

These first few minutes of the lesson help students become engaged in the learning process. It also helps to give them ownership of their own learning.

There are various ways to state and communicate the learning intention to students. I usually like to say, "We are learning how to…" and then state the learning intention. Here are a few other sentence starters you can use to state your learning intention to students:

- We are learning how to …

- Students will be able to …

- I am learning how to …

- We will be able to …

Now, take a look at the following learning intentions and come up with a hook or anticipatory set. How can you engage students in learning them? How can you keep it concise, intentional, and connected?

STANDARD: CCSS.MATH.CONTENT.5.NBT.A.4 — 5TH GRADE	
Use place value understanding to round decimals to any place.	
Learning Intention	We are learning how to round decimals.
Hook	

STANDARD: CCSS.ELA-LITERACY.RL.1.3 — 1ST GRADE	
Describe characters, settings, and major events in a story, using key details.	
Learning Intention	We are learning how to describe characters in a story using key details.
Hook	

STANDARD: CCSS.ELA-LITERACY.SL.3.3 — 3RD GRADE	
Ask and answer questions about information from a speaker, offering appropriate elaboration and detail.	
Learning Intention	We are learning how to ask and answer questions about information from a speaker using detail and elaboration.
Hook	

LEVELS OF UNDERSTANDING

Another effective way to improve student and teacher communication while building a strong relationship is by incorporating the use of levels of understanding (Marzano et al., 2017, 29):

Level 4: I totally understand this and can teach my peers.

Level 3: I almost have it, but I may need a little more practice.

Level 2: I am a little confused and need some clarification.

Level 1: I am lost. Please reteach me.

It is important to teach students what each level means and what each level might look like while learning a new skill. After students feel comfortable identifying which level they're at during the learning progression, they can share this information with you.

I usually have my students use their hands to hold up a number that represents their level of understanding throughout the lesson. They can also write their level directly on their work, a piece of scratch paper, or on their whiteboards for you to check. We'll cover this in more depth in Chapter 8.

SELF-ASSESSMENT

Self-assessment is another empowering tool for students. A few years ago, my administrators and I developed something called a Self-Assessment Ticket. Using these Self-Assessment Tickets supported my students' learning, as well as our student-Teacher partnership. It added another layer of communication between my students and me. I knew how they felt about a learning intention and whether or not their level of understanding grew, stayed the same, or even lowered during the lesson.

In the example on page 27, Maya already had a strong understanding of the learning intention. Based on her progress during independent practice and her reflection, I knew that Maya needed extension practice to further challenge her.

Once students become more comfortable with this process, their reflections and self-assessment become more authentic.

The tickets also develop a starting point for conversations about learning between the student and the teacher.

We'll go into more detail about how to implement the use of Self-Assessment Tickets in your classroom when we get to Chapter 8.

See page 138 for a version of a Self-Assessment Ticket that you can copy for your own use.

SUMMARY

Positive student-teacher relationships help students succeed, take ownership of their learning, and achieve more of their goals in school, yielding a .74 effect size (Hattie 2012, 266). This equates to almost two years' growth in a year's time. Spend more time creating meaningful learning intentions that connect with student experiences, and make sure to include opportunities for students to voice their level of understanding throughout your lessons. Constant two-way communication and feedback are key.

Name _Maya_   Date _1/20/21_

LEARNING OBJECTIVE

We are learning how to create unit fractions

SELF-ASSESSMENT

	I totally understand and can teach my peers. (4)	I almost have it, but I may need a little more practice. (3)	I am a little confused and need some clarification. (2)	I am lost. Please reteach me. (1)
Before Lesson	✔			
After Lesson	✔			
Teacher Analysis	✔			

REFLECTION

- I feel …
- I know …
- My goal is …
- I enjoyed …
- I did not like …
- I would like it if …
- I need help with …
- I am worried about …
- Next, I would like to …
- What I liked about this lesson was …

UNDERSTANDING

I feel very happy because I learned more fractions

CHAPTER 3

PROGRESSION OF LEARNING

When I was growing up, there was so much emphasis on earning certain letter grades. In elementary school, the goal was to earn an O for "outstanding work," and in secondary school, I was always so focused on getting that A. I always felt the pressure to be in the advanced reading group or the advanced math group because, let's face it, all the students know who's in each group. Unfortunately, this emphasis on the letter grade is still prevalent today.

It wasn't until I became a teacher that I realized the letter grade really isn't all that powerful. What good is an A if your students are just going to forget the material or skills after the test?

Shifting my thinking to progress over perfection created a whole new way to plan instruction and support my students. This involves taking more formative assessments, collaborating with my grade-level team, and intentionally involving students in the learning and planning process, all of which are described in the upcoming pages. It also transformed the way I structured my leveled groups to fluidly transition students from one group to another depending on the skill we're working on or reviewing.

This helps to ensure that students won't feel the stigma of being in one group over another.

Learning is a progression toward a goal. As teachers, when we focus on the progression of learning, we're helping students master their understanding of particular skills and objectives. If even just a little progress is made, it MUST be celebrated!

FORMATIVE ASSESSMENTS

Formative assessment consists of using data to help teachers improve their instructional practice. I use formative assessment to help me understand each student's learning progression toward the learning goal or learning intention. There are many ways to do this, from using whiteboards, exit tickets, and the **think-pair-share strategy**, where students first think about their response, pair up with someone near them, and then turn and talk with that partner, to using levels of understanding, progress monitoring, and individual check-ins. Such strategies help guide students to master the material rather than just obtain a letter grade. We'll explore the areas of formative assessment more closely in Chapter 8.

Formative assessment results should not be kept to yourself but shared with your students through feedback. This helps them become more aware of their own learning and shifts their mindset to be more goal oriented. The partnership between the teacher and the student, as well as the positive communication between them, helps both parties understand where to go next.

COLLABORATION WITH COLLEAGUES

For so long, teachers have gone into their classroom, closed the door, and taught in isolation. This method does not help ALL students. Whenever even one teacher changes their mindset to favor the progression of learning over a system of earning letter grades, they should share this mindset with their grade-level team. Think about how confusing it is for students to adapt from one teaching and learning style to another as they move from class to class! We often think about those in our class as only our students, but how much more of an impact we could make if we thought of ALL of those in our grade level or school as our students.

As mentioned in Chapter 1, collaboration with colleagues is one of the most powerful tools to increase student achievement. When teachers share ideas, data, and learning intentions and plan together, it helps everyone. As John Hattie said in *Visible Learning for Teachers*, "Sharing a common understanding of progression is the most critical success factor in any school."

To help foster the progression of learning mindset, it is important for grade-level teams to plan together, administer the same formative assessments, and disaggregate data from those formative assessments to help all of their students. We'll look more at deconstructing standards and what this sort of intentional planning looks like in Chapter 4.

INVOLVING STUDENTS IN THE LEARNING PROCESS

Every teacher tries to develop a sense of community in their classroom. One way to strengthen your classroom community is to make sure you're intentionally involving students in the learning process.

Students should have a clear understanding that their learning is a progression and that mistakes are normal. They should also be aware that their goal should not be an A grade but rather a full and complex understanding of the information being taught.

Here are some ways you can support your students to understand and be aware of their learning progression.

DEMONSTRATE AND PROMOTE A GROWTH MINDSET

Having a growth mindset is key to measuring progression in learning. Things can be hard. There can be setbacks. And that's okay!

I like to give my students opportunities to think about their growth mindset while also reminding them that it's okay to fail sometimes. With a growth mindset, students can reach their learning goals with more positivity and perseverance.

Growth-mindset exit tickets are helpful to use at the end of the day or even after a challenging activity or lesson. Students can write about what inspired them that day or during the lesson, how they showed perseverance, and what challenges they were able to embrace. Having students reflect on their challenges and how they handled obstacles will support them in overcoming future challenges.

	Inspiration I used today:	
	Perseverance helped me today:	
	Challenges I embraced today:	

See page 140 for a version of this growth-mindset exit ticket that you can copy for your own use.

POSITIVE WORDS AND POSITIVE MINDS

Another quick writing activity I ask students to complete as they reflect on their learning and progress toward mastery is my Powerful Words! bookmark activity. Students list 10 positive words, write about something that happened that was great, write about a mistake they made, and then choose one word that they'll refer to for the rest of the day as they focus on positivity.

POWERFUL WORDS!

THINK POSITIVELY!

1. ....   6. ....

2. ....   7. ....

3. ....   8. ....

4. ....   9. ....

5. ....   10. ....

WHAT HAPPENED THAT WAS GREAT?!

....

....

WHAT MISTAKES DID YOU MAKE?

....

....

....

POSITIVE WORD FOR THE DAY

....

See page 141 for a version of the Powerful Words! bookmark that you can copy for your own use.

EMBRACE THE LEARNING CHALLENGE, ESPECIALLY THE LEARNING PIT

The Learning Challenge was first created by James Nottingham, the cofounder and director of Challenging Learning, an education company that helps strengthen education for young people by working with educators around the world with professional development opportunities, including keynote speakers and consultation. The Learning Challenge helps students think and talk about learning by promoting "challenge, dialogue, and a growth mindset." When students talk about their own learning, it helps them to understand the progress they are making.

At the center of the Learning Challenge is the **Learning Pit**. According to Nottingham, a learner enters the Learning Pit when they've "uncovered lots of examples and exceptions" to the concept, and they've realized that it's pretty complex (Nottingham et al. 2018, 5). This is where deep learning begins to take place.

When students enter the Learning Pit, it is important to remind them about the deep learning that is taking place. Students may get frustrated or want to give up, but this is your opportunity as a teacher to remind them to keep a growth mindset, overcome the Learning Pit, and eventually reach the *eureka* stage of the Learning Challenge when they feel a sense of understanding and the satisfaction of learning. It is important to celebrate when students persevere through the Learning Pit, acknowledging that it pays off to work through challenges.

I have had great success introducing the Learning Challenge concept to my students and having honest conversations with them about being willing to admit when they're struggling or avoiding something they think is too hard. Such conversations create a stronger teacher-student relationship as students feel comfortable sharing their fears or being unable to process learning a certain skill in that moment. This creates an opportunity for students to lower their affective filter, or negative feelings toward learning, and be more willing to put in the work in order to reach the *eureka* phase of the Learning Challenge.

EMPOWER STUDENTS WITH FEEDBACK

Feedback from the teachers allows the student to be in the driver's seat of his or her learning. When students are in control of their learning, it gives them more ownership of learning goals and more motivation to meet or exceed standards .

As teachers, we often talk about **extrinsic motivation**, or using external factors to learn and be engaged in lessons. At the onset, positive feedback may act as an extrinsic motivator. But this will soon turn into **intrinsic motivation**, where the students are motivated by their own goals and desires to improve and move forward in their learning.

As the classroom teacher, you can give your students feedback in many ways. You can hold writing conferences and use success criteria as the basis of your conference. Ask your students to reflect on their writing while also linking it to the success criteria. For example, if students are writing an opinion piece, they may use the following as success criteria while they're writing (use the Success Criteria template for opinion writing on page 144):

- I can support my opinion with reasons.

- I can support my opinion with examples.

- I can use details from different texts to support my opinion.

- I can use details from my personal experiences to support my opinion.

- I can cite evidence from different texts using "What does the text say?" starters.

- I can use opinion-writing signal words.

When you conference with students, you can ask them to reflect on the success criteria and where they might find those elements in their writing. If they are not able to locate a criterion, then this would be a good opportunity to ask your students how they could improve their writing to include that element.

While reading, you can ask students to reflect on and communicate about how they're able to locate information in a text. To practice **explicit comprehension** while reading, students would answer questions by locating information in the text, looking for main ideas and supporting ideas, and pointing to explicit evidence that they can use to support their thinking. Through these activities, students can self-reflect, assessing their progress on independently finding information from a text.

If you've taught a lesson on how to find the main idea and supporting details, then students can refer back to the steps of that lesson to self-assess their progress as they work independently. Here is an example of what steps for a lesson on finding the main idea might look like:

1. Read the text.

2. Determine the overall topic of the text; highlight the text if necessary.

3. Identify and underline supporting details that explain the main idea.

4. Ask yourself, "Do the details I identified support the main idea?"

To practice **inferential comprehension** strategies, students work on using their own experiences and previous knowledge, as well as drawing from evidence from the text, to make inferences, or conclusions, about characters, plot, or other story details. As they make progress toward mastering inferential comprehension, they can self-assess by asking themselves if they have textual evidence or prior knowledge or experience to support their inference.

If you've taught a lesson to your students about making inferences, it might also be helpful for them to refer back to the steps of your lesson to self-assess. Here is an example of what the steps to an inferential comprehension lesson might look like:

1. After reading the question, refer back to the text.

2. Look for textual evidence that will help you make an inference (guess).

3. Think about what you already know or about any past experiences that can help you make an inference to support your thinking.

4. Ask yourself, "Do the details I identified support my inference?"

Communicating their ideas and how they access content can give students a clearer picture of how they learn. During math, feedback can consist of asking students to think aloud about how they reached the answer to the problem and explaining the different strategies they used to get their answer. Bringing questions back to the student can also help facilitate a conversation in which they come to an understanding of where something may have gone right or wrong.

You can facilitate this type of conversation through Math Talk activities. Equip students with sentence frames to help them articulate their thinking about math, identify where they are in the progression of learning a math topic, support one another, and ask questions while in math groups.

Sentence frames to explain and justify my work:

- Another way to solve is _____.
- I know this is true because _____.
- I can justify my answer by _____.
- From my point of view, the answer is _____ because _____.
- I can compare my answer to _____ because _____.
- I was able to identify the answer by _____.

Sentence frames to justify a peer's solution:

- Why do you think that?
- Do you think that _____?
- Can you justify your answer?
- Please analyze the answer by _____.
- Demonstrate how you were able to solve, please.

Sentence frames to clarify a peer's solution:

- Can you please give me an example?
- Can you tell me more?
- Can you explain that to me?
- Can you demonstrate how you solved the problem?

Sentence frames for sharing ideas with a peer:

- I agree with you because _____.
- I respectfully disagree with you because _____.

When students have the opportunity to think about math, talk about math, and listen to math ideas from peers, it gives them a new perspective on understanding math concepts.

SELF-REFLECTION ON THE LEARNING PROGRESSION

As you bring the principles of teacher clarity into the classroom, it's important to provide your students with ample time and resources to self-reflect.

If students can reflect on their learning and pose questions, it promotes clarity about the lesson, activity, or assessment, as well as their understanding toward the progression of the learning goals.

Here are a few sentence frames to help foster self-reflection during the progression of learning:

- I understand _____ because _____ .

- I am still unsure about _____ .

- My understanding has increased about today's lesson because _____ .

- I still have a few questions about _____ . They are _____ .

- My effort today was _____ .

- Tomorrow I will try _____ .

- My growth mindset today was _____ .

- I need help with _____ .

SUMMARY

Learning isn't just about a letter grade. It is about progressing toward meeting and exceeding the learning intention. Students' progress toward a learning goal should be celebrated at every moment, even if it happens in small steps. To help students be more aware in their learning progression, encourage them to keep a growth mindset, stay positive, and offer feedback about their learning and the work and progress they have already made throughout the lesson or unit.

CHAPTER 4

DECONSTRUCTING STANDARDS

Your school site provides books and boxed curriculum resources to help support you in teaching the state's standards. In order to help your students make progress toward meeting those standards, however, it is essential to know and understand what they entail.

The state standards can be overwhelming and, oftentimes, one standard alone can have two to three learning objectives. So how do we as teachers go about ensuring that we understand what the standards are asking of our students? It is essential to deconstruct each standard and truly identify the learning objectives that are written into them.

This chapter will look at these steps for deconstructing a standard:

1. Identify the individual sentences of the standard.

2. Identify the key phrases, words, or academic vocabulary that students will need to understand and be familiar with for the lesson.

3. Identify the actions or verbs listed in the standard.

4. Use the sentences, key phrases, and actions identified to create a learning intention.

INDIVIDUAL SENTENCES

Let's start with a 3rd-grade math standard.

STANDARD: CCSS.MATH.CONTENT.3.OA.D.8

Solve two-step word problems using the four operations. Represent these problems using equations with a letter standing for the unknown quantity. Assess the reasonableness of answers using mental computation and estimation strategies including rounding.

This standard is limited to problems posed with whole numbers and having whole-number answers; students should know how to perform operations in conventional order when there are no parentheses to specify a particular order (Order of Operations).

Let's first list all of the independent sentences of the standard.

- Solve two-step word problems using the four operations.

- Represent these problems using equations with a letter standing for the unknown quantity.

- Assess the reasonableness of answers using mental computation and estimation strategies including rounding.

- Students should know how to perform operations in conventional order when there are no parentheses to specify a particular order.

KEY PHRASES AND TERMS

Now let's go back to identify the key phrases and terms in each sentence from the standard. Students will need to know and understand these during the lesson in order to make progress or meet the standard.

Sentence from Standard: Solve two-step word problems using the four operations.	
Key Words and Phrases	• *two-step word problems* • *four operations*

Sentence from Standard: Represent these problems using equations with a letter standing for the unknown quantity.	
Key Words and Phrases	• *equations with letter standing for the unknown quantity*

Sentence from Standard: Assess the reasonableness of answers using mental computation and estimation strategies including rounding.	
Key Words and Phrases	• *reasonableness* • *mental computation* • *estimation strategies* • *rounding*

Sentence from Standard: Students should know how to perform operations in conventional order when there are no parentheses to specify a particular order.	
Key Words and Phrases	• *operations* • *conventional order*

ACTIONS/VERBS

Now let's pull out the actions or verbs that students will need to complete in order to make progress or meet the standard. The actions will help us develop our learning objectives and intentions, and assess and monitor student progress throughout the lesson. They are what the students will have to complete during the lesson.

Sentence from Standard: Solve two-step word problems using the four operations.	
Key Words and Phrases	• *two-step word problems* • *four operations*
Actions and Verbs	• *solve* • *using*

Sentence from Standard: Represent these problems using equations with a letter standing for the unknown quantity.	
Key Words and Phrases	• *equations with letter standing for the unknown quantity*
Actions and Verbs	• *represent*

Sentence from Standard: Assess the reasonableness of answers using mental computation and estimation strategies including rounding.	
Key Words and Phrases	• *reasonableness* • *mental computation* • *estimation strategies* • *rounding*
Actions and Verbs	• *assess* • *using* • *rounding*

Sentence from Standard: Students should know how to perform operations in conventional order when there are no parentheses to specify a particular order.	
Key Words and Phrases	• *operations*
Actions and Verbs	• *perform*

LEARNING INTENTIONS

Finally, after identifying the key words/phrases and actions/verbs, we're ready to create our learning intentions. I prefer using the phrase "We are learning how to…" instead of "I can" statements because sometimes students are still learning by the end of the lesson, and they may not be able to say that they "can" do it yet. Learning is all about progress, not perfection.

Here's a look at the learning intentions for this 3rd-grade math standard:

STANDARD: CCSS.MATH.CONTENT.3.OA.D.8
Solve two-step word problems using the four operations. Represent these problems using equations with a letter standing for the unknown quantity. Assess the reasonableness of answers using mental computation and estimation strategies including rounding.

Sentence from Standard: Solve two-step word problems using the four operations.	
Key Words and Phrases	• *two-step word problems* • *four operations*
Actions and Verbs	• *solve* • *using*

Learning Intentions	• We are learning how to solve two-step word problems using the four operations.
Sentence from Standard: Represent these problems using equations with a letter standing for the unknown quantity.	
Key Words and Phrases	• equations with letter standing for the unknown quantity
Actions and Verbs	• represent
Learning Intentions	• We are learning how to represent equations with a letter standing for the unknown quantity.
Sentence from Standard: Assess the reasonableness of answers using mental computation and estimation strategies including rounding.	
Key Words and Phrases	• reasonableness • mental computation • estimation strategies • rounding
Actions and Verbs	• assess • using • rounding
Learning Intention	• We are learning how to assess the reasonableness of answers using mental computation. • We are learning how to assess the reasonableness of answers using estimation strategies.
Sentence from Standard: Students should know how to perform operations in conventional order when there are no parentheses to specify a particular order.	
Key Words and Phrases	• operations
Actions and Verbs	• perform
Learning Intention	• We are learning how to perform operations in the correct order using Order of Operations.

After deconstructing this standard and being sure to look at the footnotes, it seems that this one particular math standard for 3rd grade has five learning intentions:

1. We are learning how to solve two-step word problems using the four operations.

2. We are learning how to represent equations with a letter standing for the unknown quantity.

3. We are learning how to assess the reasonableness of answers using mental computation.

4. We are learning how to assess the reasonableness of answers using estimation strategies.

5. We are learning how to perform operations in the correct order using Order of Operations.

Now let's try deconstructing an English Language Arts Standard for 5th grade.

STANDARD: **CCSS.ELA-LITERACY.RI.5.1**
Quote accurately from a text when explaining what the text says explicitly and when drawing inferences from the text.

Sentence from Standard: Quote accurately from the text when explaining what the text says.	
Key Words and Phrases	• *accurately* • *text*
Actions and Verbs	• *quote* • *explaining*
Learning Intention	• *We are learning how to quote accurately from the text when explaining what the text says.*

Sentence from Standard: Quote accurately from the text when drawing inferences from the text.	
Key Words and Phrases	• *accurately* • *text*
Actions and Verbs	• *quote* • *drawing inferences*
Learning Intention	• *We are learning how to quote accurately from the text when drawing inferences from the text.*

SUMMARY

Deconstructing standards is the core of effective instruction. It is extremely important to understand what the standards are asking of our students if we want to create and execute strong and valuable lessons.

See page 142 for a Deconstructing Standards Template that you can copy and use.

CHAPTER 5

DEVELOPING SUCCESS CRITERIA

In the previous chapter, we dove into deconstructing and analyzing standards to see what they are asking of our students. In doing this we are able to communicate clear learning intentions to our students. This gives clarity to a lesson and help students make progress toward meeting or exceeding the standard.

Let's review the steps for deconstructing standards and creating a learning intention:

1. Identify the individual sentences from the standard.

2. Identify the key phrases or words that students will need to understand and be familiar with for the lesson.

3. Identify the actions or verbs listed in the standard.

4. Use the sentences, key phrases, and actions you identified to create a learning intention.

STEPS TO CREATE THE SUCCESS CRITERIA

Now let's take a look at learning intentions and determine the steps needed to create the success criteria tied to them.

Success criteria provide students with an opportunity to assess their own learning, a process called **assessment as learning**. Assessment as learning occurs when students use the feedback from personally monitoring what they're learning to make adjustments, adaptations, and even major changes in what they understand.

For example, let's say that Jacob is writing a narrative and needs some support adding elements to make it more robust. He can look back at the success criteria for narrative pieces and compare them to what he has written. This will help him monitor his progress and assess what he has completed or still needs to complete in order to be successful. Success criteria for narrative writing might look something like this:

- I can write a strong lead that grabs the reader's attention.

- I can write in the correct sequence of events.

- I can write a problem and solution in a narrative.

- I can use dialogue with the appropriate punctuation.

- I can describe characters using their feelings, traits, motivations, and actions.

- I can write a strong conclusion that explains how the story's problem was solved.

According to *The Teacher Clarity Playbook: A Hands-On Guide to Creating Learning Intentions and Success Criteria for Organized, Effective Instruction*, "Success criteria let students in on the secret that has been too often kept from them—what the destination looks like." The success criteria help students and teachers monitor progress toward learning, in turn making learning visible to both parties.

Students can gauge their progress toward learning while completing an independent practice assignment. Here is another example of success criteria during an independent math practice assignment. Let's say that Joshua is working on renaming or decomposing mixed numbers in order to subtract. To make sure he is following the correct steps and understanding the concept, Joshua can use success criteria. Success criteria for subtracting mixed numbers by renaming or decomposing might look like the following:

- I can find the lowest common denominator of two fractions.

- I can decompose mixed numbers by taking apart the whole number.

- I can add and subtract fractions with uncommon denominators.

- I can add and subtract fractions with common denominators.

- I can simplify fractions.

Different types of success criteria can be created to help students understand what meeting the learning intention will entail. Success criteria can be "I can" statements that are tied to the learning intention. These might consist of more than one statement per learning intention. Success criteria might also include statements about what has already been learned in the lesson (Nottingham et al. 2018, 31), as shown below.

Learning Intention: We are learning how to determine literal and nonliteral word meanings.

Success Criteria:

- I can use context clues to determine word meanings.

- I can explain the literal word meaning.

- I can explain the nonliteral word meaning.

- I can explain why an author would use nonliteral language.

For longer tasks, success criteria might look like a rubric. A strong rubric should give students multiple opportunities to gauge their own progress, using indicators and performance descriptors that students can use to monitor their success.

INFORMATIVE WRITING RUBRIC	
Score	Purpose and Organization
4	The writing piece is extremely clear and organized. • The main idea is clearly stated and explained throughout the writing piece. • The main idea is supported by strong key details. • There is a strong use of transitional words to identify the relationship between ideas. • There is a strong introduction and strong conclusion. • Ideas are written in the correct sequence of events. • There is a strong variety of sentence types. • Evidence is cited and accurately quoted throughout the writing piece.

3	The writing piece is clear and organized.
	• The main idea is stated in the writing piece.
	• The main idea is supported by key details.
	• There is use of transitional words to identify the relationship between ideas.
	• There is an introduction and conclusion.
	• Ideas are written in the correct sequence of events.
	• There is a variety of sentence types.
	• Evidence is cited throughout the writing piece.
2	The writing piece is somewhat clear.
	• The main idea is somewhat clear.
	• The main idea is somewhat stated by key details.
	• There is use a weak use of transitional words to identify the relationship between ideas.
	• Ideas are written out of order and the writing piece does not have a consistent flow of ideas.
	• There is limited variety of sentence usage.
	• Evidence is not cited throughout the writing piece.
1	The writing piece is not clear
	• The main idea is not clear
	• The main idea is not supported by key details.
	• There are no transitional words to identify the relationship between ideas.
	• Ideas are written out of order and the writing piece does not have a consistent flow of ideas.
	• There is no variety of sentence usage.
	• Evidence is not cited throughout the writing piece.

Success criteria should *not* consist of tasks to be completed; e.g., "Complete the science lab" or "Finish the essay." Those statements do not help or support students in understanding the learning intention (Fisher et al. 2018, 30).

Now let's look at how we can create our own success criteria that are linked to the learning intentions created in the previous chapter.

STANDARD: CCSS.MATH.CONTENT.3.OA.D.8

Solve two-step word problems using the four operations. Represent these problems using equations with a letter standing for the unknown quantity. Assess the reasonableness of answers using mental computation and estimation strategies including rounding.

After deconstructing this particular standard, we developed five learning intentions:

1. We are learning how to solve two-step word problems using the four operations.

2. We are learning how to represent equations with a letter standing for the unknown quantity.

3. We are learning how to assess the reasonableness of answers using mental computation.

4. We are learning how to assess the reasonableness of answers using estimation strategies.

5. We are learning how to perform operations in the correct order using Order of Operations.

Let's start by looking at the first learning intention and determining what students need to know before acquiring this new skill. In order to solve two-step word problems using the four operations, students would need to know what the four operations are and how to solve the operations in the correct order. If it is determined that your students already know those skills, then those can be a part of your success criteria.

Example:

Learning Intention	• *We are learning how to solve two-step word problems using the four operations.*

Success Criteria	• *I can identify the four operations used in math to solve problems.*
	
	• *I can use the Order of Operations to solve word problems.*
	
	• *I can use CUBES to solve word problems.*
	
	    C—Circle the numbers
	    U—Underline the question
	    B—Box the action words
	    E—Eliminate the unnecessary
	    S—Solve and explain
	
	• *I can solve one-step word problems using CUBES.*

Remember, success criteria support students in understanding what they'll need to do in order to meet the learning intention. If your students have not mastered the skills that are listed in the success criteria, then they won't be able to meet the new learning intention. For example, in the success criteria listed above, students must already have experience using CUBES or the Order of Operations. If you've determined that they do not have experience in those skills, you may have to develop another learning intention to teach those skills before going into this learning intention. Your new learning intention might be, "We are learning how to use the Order of Operations to solve number sentences."

Now let's take a look at the second learning intention for this standard:

Learning Intention	• *We are learning how to represent equations with a letter standing for the unknown quantity.*

Let's ask ourselves what skills students will need to know or what they already know in order to meet this standard. These include adding and subtracting without using a letter for the unknown or understanding the academic vocabulary term "variable."

Some appropriate success criteria for this learning intention might be:

Learning Intention	• We are learning how to represent equations with a letter standing for the unknown quantity.
Success Criteria	• I can add and subtract. I can use variables to represent the unknown quantity in an equation.

Here's the third learning intention:

Learning Intention	• We are learning how to assess the reasonableness of answers using mental computation.

Let's ask ourselves what skills students will need to know or what they already know in order to meet this standard. These include mental math strategies, skip counting, rounding, and determining compatible numbers.

Some appropriate success criteria for this learning intention might be:

Learning Intention	• We are learning how to assess the reasonableness of answers using mental computation

Success Criteria	• *I can use mental math to add and subtract.*
	• *I can use compatible numbers to round mentally.*
	• *I can skip count to add and subtract mentally.*

Now try creating success criteria for the last two learning intentions:

Learning Intention	• *We are learning how to assess the reasonableness of answers using estimation strategies.*

Learning Intention	• *We are learning how to perform operations in the correct order using Order of Operations.*

Which skills will students need to know or what have they already learned that will support them in progressing toward mastery for this learning intention?

Learning Intention	• *We are learning how to assess the reasonableness of answers using estimation strategies.*
Success Criteria	

Learning Intention	• *We are learning how to perform operations in the correct order using Order of Operations.*
Success Criteria	

Here are some examples of success criteria and learning intentions:

LEARNING INTENTION	SUCCESS CRITERIA
We are learning how to support the main idea.	• *I determined the main idea.* • *I cited enough evidence from the text to support the main idea.* • *I included specific examples from the text.* • *I used "What does the text say?" starters in my response.* • *My answer uses evidence from the text, and it is clearly explained.*
We are learning how to determine the central message of a story.	• *I can determine the message or theme of the story.* • *I can support my ideas with details from the text.* • *I can cite evidence to support my ideas.* • *I can use the sequence of events to explain the central message.*
We are learning how to add fractions with uncommon denominators.	• *I can add and subtract fractions with common denominators.* • *I can use multiples to find the least common multiple.* • *I can use multiplication to find equivalent fractions.* • *I can simplify improper fractions and convert them to mixed numbers.*

SUMMARY

Success criteria help students understand the learning intention and give them a clear pathway to meet the learning intention. Success criteria are not tasks to be completed, but rather they are skills students can do to meet the new learning goal. Success criteria can be part of the "big idea" of your lesson, and they can also be structured to fit what students may already know coming into the lesson.

See pages 144 to 145 for examples of success criteria templates for narrative writing.

CHAPTER 6

EXPLICIT INSTRUCTION

Let's take a look back at all that you have done to bring teacher clarity into your classroom. You've deconstructed standards and created learning intentions and success criteria. You've also developed ways to give your students feedback, nurture positive teacher-student relationships, and cultivate a classroom culture that promotes and celebrates each student's progression toward mastering the learning goal.

Now it's time to teach!

Explicit instruction, or **direct instruction**, is an effective teaching practice that clearly communicates learning intentions and success criteria to students. Madeline Hunter first developed the direct instruction model, also known as instructional theory, into a practice teaching model. It includes seven components: objectives, standards, anticipatory set, teaching (input, modeling, checking for understanding), guided practice/ monitoring, closure, and independent practice (Wikimedia 2005).

The term "direct instruction" may cause some teachers to think that the delivery of instruction will be rigid, boring, and mundane. This is not true! The form of direct instruction I am about to introduce to you can be tailored to fit your teaching style while also incorporating student collaboration, clear modeling, and a chance to differentiate for all students while teaching. Direct instruction yields a 0.59 effect size, which is more than a year's growth in a year's time (Hattie 2016, 47). When the key elements of direct instruction are used and executed properly, it promotes teacher clarity, engages students, and helps them progress toward their learning goals.

To plan a direct instruction lesson, it's important to determine the type of learning that is taking place. There are two types of lesson designs to consider as you begin to write your lesson. Will students need to *know* something (**declarative**) or will students need to *do* something (**procedural**)?

Declarative knowledge examples include vocabulary, facts, principles, and concepts. Procedural knowledge involves rules, steps, and other combination procedures.

Whether you're teaching a declarative or procedural lesson, both lessons should contain the following elements.

HOOK

The hook is the onset of the lesson and should grab students' attention. You may have even heard of it as the "anticipatory set." The hook aims to quickly engage students in what you're about to teach so they'll be ready to learn and actively participate in the lesson.

LEARNING INTENTION

As we've discussed, the learning intention is the learning goal students are working toward mastering. You developed strong learning intentions, also known as "learning objectives" or "learning goals," earlier in the book by deconstructing standards and isolating skills.

After the hook portion of your lesson, have students state the learning intention. It will provide them clarity and ensure that they know the goal of the lesson. This is also the time when I ask students to rate their level of understanding to see how they feel before we start the lesson. I also ask them at the end of the lesson so they can reflect on how they've grown or areas where they still need support.

REVIEW

When teaching a direct instruction lesson, it's important to review skills that correspond with the new skill or learning goal. This part of the lesson should be short and sweet, and it should also be easy for students to connect the ideas together.

BIG IDEA

Students often ask why they need to learn something, or why certain skills are being taught in school. The big idea component of the direct instruction model offers students an explanation and the "why" behind the learning intention. Take this time during the explanation of the big idea to link to real-world applications, previously taught vocabulary, or connections students may have to the learning intention. This should be more than just "You'll be tested on this in the spring." Students need to have a deeper connection and understanding of the learning goal so they'll be more invested in the learning progression.

MODEL

The model portion of the lesson can look different for a procedural than it does for a declarative lesson. To recap, in a procedural lesson, students are learning how to do something. In a declarative lesson, students are learning about something.

Model a procedural lesson by clearly and explicitly going through the steps that students will need to complete. It is important for students to have a clear model of what they need to do in order for them to successfully practice it themselves. This type of model can include steps, too. Here's an example of steps for a math learning intention:

Learning intention: We are learning how to add fractions with uncommon denominators.

1. Determine the denominators.

2. Find the lowest common denominator (LCD) by listing the multiples of each denominator.

3. Change the denominators after you find the LCD.

4. Add the numerators.

5. Simplify, if necessary.

As you are modeling, consistently refer back to the steps. Modeling two example problems would be helpful for students to see before they practice on their own.

When teaching a declarative lesson, a graphic organizer or a model of how to search for information in a text can be really helpful. Here's an example of a declarative model for a social studies learning intention:

> We are learning how to explain the struggle American Indian leaders had in the fight for their land against European settlers.

Steps would not work well for this learning intention, but coming up with a mnemonic device to help students remember the information would be beneficial. For this particular learning intention, my students were learning about three leaders: Tah-gah-jute, Chief Tecumseh, and Chief John Ross. I decided to make a mnemonic device for students to remember those three names. I came up with "Together Through Justice." The first letter of each word was meant to help them remember the first letter of each of the American Indian leaders' names.

I used a graphic organizer like this one to record our ideas as we learned about each leader's struggle:

TAH-GAH-JUTE (TOGETHER)	CHIEF TECUMSEH (THROUGH)	CHIEF JOHN ROSS (JUSTICE)

Throughout the lesson and as we read informational text together, we filled in the graphic organizer to explain and connect back to the learning intention: how each leader fought for their land against European settlers.

By the end of the lesson, our graphic organizer looked like this:

TAH-GAH-JUTE (TOGETHER)	CHIEF TECUMSEH (THROUGH)	CHIEF JOHN ROSS (JUSTICE)
At first, Tah-gah-jute (Logan) helped settlers who moved into the Ohio River Valley. His family was killed by colonial traders. Then he led the Mingo and their allies (the Shawnee) in attacks against settlers. Governor of Virginia (Lord Dunmore) sent troops to the area, and Logan was defeated. A treaty was created and American Indians would need to give up their land; Logan refused to sign.	A Shawnee leader (early 1800s) who attempted to bring American Indian groups together to oppose migration of settlers into the MS and OH River Valleys. A great speaker, he convinced many to become allies against settlers. Some American Indian leaders signed treaties that gave up land, and he demanded the land be returned. In the Battle of Tippecanoe, US troops defeated Tecumseh's followers. In the War of 1812, Tecumseh was killed fighting against US.	He decided to seek justice without violence. He asked the US Supreme Court to stop the state of Georgia from taking control of Cherokee lands. In 1832, Chief Justice John Marshall ruled in favor of the Cherokee. President Jackson refused to support the decision of the court. 1838 troops forced the Cherokees to move west (Trail of Tears).

GUIDED PRACTICE

Guided practice, also known as the **gradual release**, is slowly leading your students to practice the newly taught skill on their own and, ultimately, practicing it independently.

Again, this may look differently for a procedural lesson than it would for a declarative lesson. In a procedural lesson for a particular skill, you gradually release students into practicing the steps as follows:

- Ask students to complete the first step with you, the second step with a partner, and the later steps on their own. Think about it as the "I do, we do, you do" model, where students aren't just thrown to the wolves, so to speak.

- As students practice the skill, check for their understanding.

- Have students write on their whiteboards, share out loud with a partner, or complete certain tasks at their seat that would be easy for you to check during a whole group lesson.

- When you feel students have grasped the concept, release them into full independent practice.

Some students may still need additional support, even after the modeling and guided practice, and that's okay! You can pull those students back to your small group table for additional scaffolding or reteaching. If your small group consists of more than three-quarters of your class, however, it would probably be a good idea to reassess your whole lesson and do a complete whole group reteach.

During a declarative lesson, the guided practice will look a little different since you won't be delivering the lesson with steps. If you were to use the example of the model I listed on page 65, you could create a guided practice for students that involves the following to ensure students are making progress toward mastering the learning intention:

- Partner talking

- Whole group conversation

- Whole group writing practice

- Sentence frames for students to fill in on their white boards while using a graphic organizer to support them in completing the questions

CLOSURE

When closing or ending a lesson, always ask students to restate the learning intention and self-assess. Has their level of understanding on the new skill increased since the beginning of the lesson? It's also imperative to ask students two to three more questions related to the lesson. The questions can be about the big idea or the success criteria. You can also ask students to complete an error analysis question, which can really help challenge their thinking.

INDEPENDENT PRACTICE

The independent practice portion of the lesson is when students complete a task on their own to ensure mastery of the skill. This offers an opportunity for the classroom teacher to assess the students' ability to complete the skill independently.

It's important to keep the students' attention spans into account, as well as make time for brain breaks and stretches. It's also essential to get to the clean model portion of your lesson (modeling the skill clearly and while thinking out loud without making mistakes or asking for student input) before you've lost your students' attention. That way, students can be in the right frame of mind for listening and learning along during the model. The following are suggested time frames for each portion of a direct instruction lesson:

- Hook (1 to 3 minutes)

- Learning Intention (1 minute)

- Review (3 to 5 minutes)

- Big Idea (3 to 5 minutes)

- Modeling (10 to 15 minutes)

- Guided Practice (10 to 15 minutes)

- Closure (1 to 3 minutes)

With a direct instruction lesson, or any type of activity, it's essential to plan with the end in mind. This helps ensure a more effective lesson because you'll have a clear idea of what you need your students to accomplish.

Ask yourself some "end in mind" planning questions:

- What do you want your students to learn from this lesson?

- What do you want your students to get out of this activity?

- What will your students need to be able to do in order to make progress toward mastery?

Here's the outline of a lesson plan in a template. Always start with the standard. Since we already deconstructed some standards in the previous chapter, let's start with one of those.

STANDARD: CCSS.MATH.CONTENT.3.OA.D.8

Solve two-step word problems using the four operations. Represent these problems using equations with a letter standing for the unknown quantity. Assess the reasonableness of answers using mental computation and estimation strategies including rounding.

This standard is limited to problems posed with whole numbers and having whole-number answers; students should know how to perform operations in conventional order when there are no parentheses to specify a particular order (Order of Operations).

Learning Intention	• We are learning how to solve two-step word problems using the four operations.
Success Criteria	• I can identify the four operations used in math to solve problems.
	• I can use the Order of Operations to solve word problems.
	• I can use CUBES to solve word problems.
	• I can solve one-step word problems using CUBES.

As a reminder, after we deconstructed this particular standard, we determined that there were a few learning intentions. I chose one of those learning intentions, listed above, to outline a procedural direct instruction lesson.

We'll use this template to create our direct instruction lesson plan. See page 143 for an Explicit Instruction Lesson Plan Template that you can copy and use.

Standard	
Hook (Make Connections)	
Learning Intention	
Review (Prior Skills)	

Big Idea (Why)	
Model (Skills, Concepts, Metacognition)	
Guided Practice	
Closure	
Independent Practice	

After deconstructing the standard, list one of the **learning intentions**.

Standard	CCSS.MATH.CONTENT.3.OA.D.8 • Solve two-step word problems using the four operations. Represent these problems using equations with a letter standing for the unknown quantity. Assess the reasonableness of answers using mental computation and estimation strategies including rounding.
Hook (Make Connections)	
Learning Intention	• We are learning how to solve two-step word problems using the four operations.
Review (Prior Skills)	
Big Idea (Why)	
Model (Skills, Concepts, Metacognition)	
Guided Practice	
Closure	

Independent Practice	

Now let's determine what students will have to complete for **independent practice** based on the learning intention.

Standard	*CCSS.MATH.CONTENT.3.OA.D.8*
	• *Solve two-step word problems using the four operations. Represent these problems using equations with a letter standing for the unknown quantity. Assess the reasonableness of answers using mental computation and estimation strategies including rounding.*
Hook (Make Connections)	
Learning Intention	• *We are learning how to solve two-step word problems using the four operations.*
Review (Prior Skills)	
Big Idea (Why)	
Model (Skills, Concepts, Metacognition)	
Guided Practice	
Closure	
Independent Practice	• *Solve four two-step word problems, one with each of the four operations. (This shows that they're identifying action words and justifying their reasoning.)*

Plan with the end in mind and ask yourself, "Does the independent practice match the learning intention?" This will help plan how to model the skill as well as check for understanding during the guided practice. If your independent practice does not match your objective, then your students will not have a clear understanding of the learning intention.

Now let's think about the skills students already know that can help them in this lesson. This will be the review portion of your instruction. The review can consist of vocabulary, a previous skill that is a foundation for learning the new skill, or something related that will remind students that they already know skills that will help them with this new learning.

Standard	CCSS.MATH.CONTENT.3.OA.D.8 • Solve two-step word problems using the four operations. Represent these problems using equations with a letter standing for the unknown quantity. Assess the reasonableness of answers using mental computation and estimation strategies including rounding.
Hook (Make Connections)	
Learning Intention	• We are learning how to solve two-step word problems using the four operations.
Review (Prior Skills)	• Examples of number sentences with adding, subtracting, multiplying, and dividing. • Examples of one-step word problems. • Examples of Order of Operations.
Big Idea (Why)	
Model (Skills, Concepts, Metacognition)	
Guided Practice	
Closure	

| Independent Practice | • *Solve four two-step word problems, one with each of the four operations. (This shows that they're identifying action words and justifying their reasoning.)* |

After determining what students will need to review before the lesson, it is important to explain the "why" behind the lesson. For the Real-World Connection, try to connect the lesson's objective to a real-world situation, making the lesson applicable for students. This is a great time to go over the success criteria related to the learning intention.

Standard	*CCSS.MATH.CONTENT.3.OA.D.8* • *Solve two-step word problems using the four operations. Represent these problems using equations with a letter standing for the unknown quantity. Assess the reasonableness of answers using mental computation and estimation strategies including rounding.*
Hook (Make Connections)	
Learning Intention	• *We are learning how to solve two-step word problems using the four operations.*
Review (Prior Skills)	• *Examples of number sentences with adding, subtracting, multiplying, and dividing.* • *Examples of one-step word problems.* • *Examples of Order of Operations.*

Big Idea (Why)	**Success Criteria** • *I can identify the four operations used in math to solve problems.* • *I can use the Order of Operations to solve word problems.* • *I can use CUBES to solve word problems.* • *I can solve one-step word problems using CUBES.* **Real-World Connection** • *Solving two-step problems happens daily as we go grocery shopping, are trying to figure out measurements for recipes and cooking, or building or creating something in our backyards or houses.*
Model (Skills, Concepts, Metacognition)	
Guided Practice	
Closure	
Independent Practice	• *Solve four two-step word problems, one with each of the four operations. (This shows that they're identifying action words and justifying their reasoning.)*

In thinking about the learning intention, how will you model this skill to your students? This is a procedural lesson, so students will be doing something. I typically include steps for students to follow in a procedural lesson, so my model would look something like this:

Standard	*CCSS.MATH.CONTENT.3.OA.D.8* • *Solve two-step word problems using the four operations. Represent these problems using equations with a letter standing for the unknown quantity. Assess the reasonableness of answers using mental computation and estimation strategies including rounding.*
Hook (Make Connections)	
Learning Intention	• *We are learning how to solve two-step word problems using the four operations.*
Review (Prior Skills)	• *Examples of number sentences with adding, subtracting, multiplying, and dividing.* • *Examples of one-step word problems.* • *Examples of Order of Operations.*
Big Idea (Why)	**Success Criteria** • *I can identify the four operations used in math to solve problems.* • *I can use the Order of Operations to solve word problems.* • *I can use CUBES to solve word problems.* • *I can solve one-step word problems using CUBES.* **Real-World Connection** • *Solving two-step problems happens daily as we go grocery shopping, are trying to figure out measurements for recipes and cooking, or building or creating something in our backyards or houses.*

Model (Skills, Concepts, Metacognition)	1. Read the word problem.
	2. Circle the numbers.
	3. Determine the action words in the word problem that will help identify the operations.
	4. Underline the question.
	5. Solve, explain, justify. (Include a model.)
	• For this particular skill, I would also use a graphic organizer to help students organize their thinking.
Guided Practice	
Closure	
Independent Practice	• Solve four two-step word problems, one with each of the four operations. (This shows that they're identifying action words and justifying their reasoning.)

Communicating and demonstrating a clear model to your students will lessen the confusion during the gradual release portion of the lesson. Start with one model, making sure to use metacognition and think-aloud strategies as you explain your thinking. Your model should not have mistakes. After going through one example, state the steps to your students. Also make sure to have the steps posted on the board or on an anchor chart so they're visible to students. They can refer back to the steps during the guided and independent practice. After stating the steps, complete one more clean model for students. I like to tell my students that the modeling time is my time to share and show my thinking strategies, and that questions can come during the guided practice.

Standard	*CCSS.MATH.CONTENT.3.OA.D.8*
	• *Solve two-step word problems using the four operations. Represent these problems using equations with a letter standing for the unknown quantity. Assess the reasonableness of answers using mental computation and estimation strategies including rounding.*
Hook (Make Connections)	
Learning Intention	• *We are learning how to solve two-step word problems using the four operations.*
Review (Prior Skills)	• *Examples of number sentences with adding, subtracting, multiplying, and dividing.*
	• *Examples of one-step word problems.*
	• *Examples of Order of Operations.*
Big Idea (Why)	***Success Criteria***
	• *I can identify the four operations used in math to solve problems.*
	• *I can use the Order of Operations to solve word problems.*
	• *I can use CUBES to solve word problems.*
	• *I can solve one-step word problems using CUBES.*
	Real-World Connection
	• *Solving two-step problems happens daily as we go grocery shopping, are trying to figure out measurements for recipes and cooking, or building or creating something in our backyards or houses.*

Model (Skills, Concepts, Metacognition)	1. Read the word problem.
	2. Circle the numbers.
	3. Determine the action words in the word problem that will help identify the operations.
	4. Underline the question.
	5. Solve, explain, justify. (Include a model.)
	• For this particular skill, I would also use a graphic organizer to help students organize their thinking.
Guided Practice	• Choose problems that students will be able to answer on their whiteboards. These problems can also be typed out on a sheet of paper and printed so that students can slip the paper into a sheet protector. Students can use their whiteboard markers to write on the sheet protector and show their work.
Closure	
Independent Practice	• Solve four two-step word problems, one with each of the four operations. (This shows that they're identifying action words and justifying their reasoning.)

After modeling two clear and concise sample problems and stating the steps explicitly, gradually release students to practice. Make sure to check for understanding throughout the release.

To release students into their practice, I might ask them to complete the first gradual release question with me as a whole group. I would continue to model my metacognition and ask for students to share their ideas with a partner and with the whole group. I might then ask students to work with a partner and complete the next questions independently. Throughout the lesson, I would constantly check for understanding through the use of whiteboards, observations, and listening to students' conversations as they talk things out with their table or group partners.

Standard	*CCSS.MATH.CONTENT.3.OA.D.8* • *Solve two-step word problems using the four operations. Represent these problems using equations with a letter standing for the unknown quantity. Assess the reasonableness of answers using mental computation and estimation strategies including rounding.*
Hook (Make Connections)	
Learning Intention	• *We are learning how to solve two-step word problems using the four operations.*
Review (Prior Skills)	• *Examples of number sentences with adding, subtracting, multiplying, dividing.* • *Examples of one-step word problems.* • *Examples of Order of Operations.*
Big Idea (Why)	**Success Criteria** • *I can identify the four operations used in math to solve problems.* • *I can use the Order of Operations to solve word problems.* • *I can use CUBES to solve word problems.* • *I can solve one-step word problems using CUBES.* **Real-World Connection** • *Solving two-step problems happens daily as we go grocery shopping, are trying to figure out measurements for recipes and cooking, or building or creating something in our backyards or houses.*

Model (Skills, Concepts, Metacognition)	1. Read the word problem.
	2. Circle the numbers.
	3. Determine the action words in the word problem that will help identify the operations.
	4. Underline the question.
	5. Solve, explain, justify. (Include a model.)
	• For this particular skill, I would also use a graphic organizer to help students organize their thinking.
Guided Practice	• Choose problems that students will be able to answer on their whiteboards. These problems can also be typed out on a sheet of paper and printed so that students can slip the paper into a sheet protector. Students can use their whiteboard markers to write on the sheet protector and show their work.
Closure	1. Restate the objective.
	2. Depth-of-Knowledge Level 2 Question.
	3. Depth-of-Knowledge Level 3 Question.
Independent Practice	• Solve four two-step word problems, one with each of the four operations. (This shows that they're identifying action words and justifying their reasoning.)

If you feel that a majority of your students have understood the learning intention and have shown progression through the gradual release, close the lesson by asking a few questions. Ask students to restate the objective, and try to include some Depth-of-Knowledge Level 2 and 3 questions into the closure so students have an opportunity to be challenged. According to the Association for Supervision and Curriculum Development (ASCD), an organization that helps support the way educators learn, Norman Webb developed the concept of the Depth of Knowledge. It was first designed as a way to increase the cognitive complexity of standardized assessments. The Depth of Knowledge supports students in thinking deeply, while also supporting them to explain their answers and how they understand concepts. There are four levels of the Depth of Knowledge:

- DOK 1-Knowledge Acquisition

- DOK 2-Knowledge Application

- DOK 3-Knowledge Analysis

- DOK 4-Knowledge Augmentation

In math, this typically looks like an error analysis question. In language arts, it can be something that students will need to infer based on the learning intention.

Notice that the hook section of the template is still blank at this point. Remember, you will write out the hook after planning the lesson.

SUMMARY

When teaching a new concept, it is essential to model the skill correctly and clearly. It is also imperative to give students time to process, practice, and apply the skill independently. Metacognition and modeling during direct instruction are key in supporting students and promoting teacher clarity. Make sure to include time for students to share with each other using structured language routines and sentence frames while also giving them time to work independently to gain confidence with the skill.

CHAPTER 7

TARGET RESPONSES

In the previous chapter, we discussed teaching with the end in mind. If we don't know what we want our students to accomplish, then how are we supposed to support them in getting there?

One effective way to plan with the end in mind is by creating **target responses**. A target response is a writing sample that has been planned out and written in advance to be used as a guide when teaching the unit or lesson. Target responses gives students the scaffolds they need to create a writing piece or culminating assignment in any subject area that meets grade-level standards.

Target responses assist all students while providing language support to English learners. It is another great strategy to help students develop their language skills and embed the various language functions within their writing.

Additionally, target responses acts as success criteria by giving students the means to assess their learning, monitor their progress, and adjust accordingly as they work toward meeting the learning goal.

HOW TO DEVELOP A TARGET RESPONSE

Let's go through how to develop a target response using a 5th-grade writing standard: CCSS.ELA-LITERACY.W.5.1: Write opinion pieces on topics or texts, supporting a point of view with reasons and information.

Let's first deconstruct the standard to determine our learning attention:

Sentence from Standard: Write an opinion piece and support your point of view with reasons and information.	
Key Words and Phrases	• opinion • point of view • reasons • information
Actions and Verbs	• write • support
Learning Intention	• We are learning how to write an opinion piece and support our point of view with reasons and information.

The success criteria I am developing for this opinion-writing task include the target response, along with the following criteria:

- I can write a strong topic sentence that introduces my opinion.

- I can use strong supporting details and examples from the text to support my reasons.

- I can cite evidence from the text to support my thinking.

- I can quote accurately from the text.

- I can write a strong conclusion that closes my opinion piece.

- I can use correct grammar and punctuation throughout my writing piece.

This writing task requires students to practice a multitude of skills, including writing a strong topic sentence and conclusion, using correct grammar, using correct punctuation, citing evidence, quoting accurately, and using supporting evidence. This unit takes about two to three weeks, to model and teach, as students will need multiple opportunities to practice and engage with the writing.

In planning with the end in mind, I first write a target response that I would expect my students to be able to write.

Here's an example:

Writing prompt: In your opinion, which makes a better pet — a cat or a dog?

I think a dog would make a better pet than a cat. Dogs are the best because they are great companions, they keep families healthy, and they are great at keeping families safe.

Dogs make great companions when they are the family pet. Dogs are patient and make great listeners, which obviously makes them a wonderful friend. They can keep secrets and can really help someone who feels lonely. They also help humans make friendships with other humans. Dogs make it easy for others to meet new people while they're out on walks.

Another reason dogs make great pets is because they keep families healthy. Studies show that dog owners are less likely to get sick. In addition, dogs also help kids stay healthy by helping their self-esteem. They make kids feel better about themselves! Since dogs need a lot of exercise, the owner will get that exercise, too. Having a dog will force the owner to stay fit.

Finally, dogs make great pets because they can help keep their families safe. Dogs will bark if there is danger. This will warn the family and help them stay alert to threats. Dogs can also scare off intruders. They can even be trained to help find missing people. Dogs are so smart, they can also sniff out bombs and help disabled people.

In conclusion, dogs make better pets than cats. They are great companions, they keep families healthy, and they are great at keeping families safe.

After writing the target response, pull out the skills you'd have to teach your students in order for them to be able to write a similar writing piece.

For this example, students would need to know:

- Incorporating opinions into paragraphs. I like to use opinion, reason, examples, opinion (OREO).

- Transition words.

- How to extract evidence from text or other media to support their thinking

- Punctuation and grammar skills. You can choose what type of language skills and lessons you'd like to embed in your writing. In this case, students would need to know how to use commas for introductory phrases, as well as commas in a series.

Considering all of the skills students will need to learn before writing, this opinion-writing unit is going to take about two to four weeks. Based on this teacher-developed target response, the following lessons need to be taught:

- **Opinion format (OREO):** CCSS.ELA-LITERACY.W.5.1.A Introduce a topic or text clearly, state an opinion, and create an organizational structure in which ideas are logically grouped to support the writer's purpose.

- **Transition words:** CCSS.ELA-LITERACY.W.5.1.C Link opinion and reasons using words, phrases, and clauses (e.g., *consequently, specifically*).

- **Gain information from multiple texts to support ideas:** CCSS.ELA-LITERACY.RI.5.9 Integrate information from several texts on the same topic in order to write or speak about the subject knowledgeably.

- **Use commas to separate introductory phrases :** CCSS.ELA-LITERACY.L.5.2.B Use a comma to separate an introductory element from the rest of the sentence.

- **Use commas to separate items in a series:** CCSS.ELA-LITERACY.L.5.2.A Use punctuation to separate items in a series.

Students will also need to know and practice using **opinion language functions**, or language that is used to write and talk about opinions. Here are a few examples:

- For instance …
- I discovered that …
- Even though …
- One of the most …
- It leads me to believe that …
- Based on …
- Due to …
- I noticed …
- Because of this …
- It makes me think that …
- In my opinion …
- I think …
- I predict …

Once you've written an example that students can strive toward meeting, then create a few more for them to use as a scaffold. I like to give my students four writing examples. I call them a Level 4 (exceeding grade level), Level 3 (grade level), Level 2 (below grade level), and Level 1 (far below grade level). This is a great way to help students self-assess and monitor their own writing progression in relation to where their writing should be for their grade level. The previous target response would be an example of a Level 3. Here are examples that I would give to my students so they can gauge their progress and success.

LEVEL 4 (EXCEEDING GRADE LEVEL):

Imagine a companion who never leaves your side, one who never ignores you or talks back to you. A companion who is always so happy to see you, no matter what differences you may have. This companion is one that you can easily have and one that is easy to care for as a pet. It is a dog. I think a dog makes the best pet, especially compared to a cat. Dogs are the best because they are great companions, they keep families healthy, and they are great at keeping families safe.

Dogs make great companions when they are the family pet. According to ehow.com, dogs are patient and make great listeners, which obviously makes them a wonderful friend. They can keep secrets and can really help someone who feels lonely. They also help humans make friendships with other humans. Cecilia McCormick, author of "Why Dogs Make Good Pets," explains that dogs make it easy for others to meet new people while they're out on walks. Cats won't do that. Cats like to stay indoors and do not want to be bothered. Why would you want a cat when they don't want to be your companion?

Another reason dogs make great pets is because they keep families healthy. Studies show that dog owners are less likely to get sick. In addition, dogs also help kids stay healthy by boosting their self-esteem. They make kids feel better about themselves! Since dogs need a lot of exercise, the owner will get that exercise, too. Having a dog will force the owner to stay fit. Cats, on the other hand, have lots of hair and sometimes get hairballs. A lot of people are also allergic to cats, and that doesn't help with your health.

Finally, dogs make great pets because they can help keep their families safe. According to the text, dogs will bark if there is danger. This will warn the family and help them stay alert to threats. Dogs can also scare off intruders. They can even be trained to help find missing people. Dogs are so smart, they can also sniff out bombs and help disabled people. Can cats do that? Nope! They just lie around on the couch, which doesn't stop an intruder from entering your house.

In conclusion, dogs make better pets than cats. They are great companions, they keep families healthy, and they are great at keeping families safe. In my opinion, dogs are the best. Do your family a favor and get a dog!

LEVEL 3 (AT GRADE LEVEL):

I think dogs would make a better pet than a cat. Dogs are the best because they are great companions, they keep families healthy, and they are great at keeping families safe.

Dogs make great companions when they are the family pet. Dogs are patient and make great listeners, which obviously makes them a wonderful friend. They can keep secrets and can really help someone who feels lonely. They also help humans make friendships with other humans. Dogs make it easy for others to meet new people while they're out on walks.

Another reason dogs make great pets is because they keep families healthy. Studies show that dog owners are less likely to get sick. In addition, dogs also help kids stay healthy by helping their self-esteem. They make kids feel better about themselves! Since dogs need a lot of exercise, the owner will also get that exercise too. Having a dog will force the owner to stay fit.

Finally, dogs make great pets because they can help keep their families safe. Dogs will bark if there is danger. This will warn the family and help them stay alert to threats. Dogs can also scare off intruders. They have even been trained to help find missing people. Dogs are so smart, they can also sniff out bombs and help disabled people.

In conclusion, dogs make better pets than cats. They are great companions, they keep families healthy, and they are great at keeping families safe.

LEVEL 2 (BELOW GRADE LEVEL):

I think a dog would make a better pet than a cat. Dogs are the best because they are great friends and they keep the family healthy. Cats don't do that because they are mean.

Dogs make good friends because they listen to you. Also, they are good friends because they help you when you are sad. Dogs are the best friends ever.

Cats aren't good friends. Dogs can keep the family healthy. Dogs make you take them on walks so they give you exercise. Cats just sit there, and cats have litter boxes.

I think dogs make better pets than cats.

LEVEL 1 (FAR BELOW GRADE LEVEL):

I think dogs and cats are great. Dogs are nice and cats are nice, too. Dogs are better than cats, though. Dogs make good friends because they listen to you. They also are good friends because they help you when you are sad. Dogs are the best friends ever. Cat's [sic] can scratch you a lot, and they are very annoying.

* * *

To give my students the access and support to write at a Level 4, I like to go back and comb through the Level 4 example to see if I need to add any other lessons to my writing unit.

The writing elements that stand out in Level 4 are a strong, attention-grabbing introduction and citing evidence from the text. I would add those two learning intentions to my unit.

Here is what my opinion-writing unit learning intentions look like so far:

- We are learning how to use OREO to write an opinion piece.

- We are learning how to link opinions and reasons using words, phrases, and clauses.

- We are learning how to gain information from multiple texts to support ideas

- We are learning how to use commas to separate introductory phrases.

- We are learning how to use commas to separate items in a series.

- We are learning how to write a strong introduction that grabs the reader's attention.

- We are learning how to cite evidence from the text to support our opinion.

Now that I know my learning intentions for the unit, I can plan these out accordingly over a period of time and have my students practice these skills using other texts. The culminating assignment will be an opinion-writing piece.

Finally, a crucial part of giving your students a target response is supporting your students with sentence frames to help guide their writing. I usually provide sentence frames to help my students when they're writing their final drafts. Here's an example of an opinion piece in sentence frames:

PARAGRAPH ONE:

(Start with an attention-grabber, such as a question, quote, or snapshot.) _____. In my opinion, _____. Three reasons to support my opinion are _____, _____, and _____.

PARAGRAPH TWO:

The first reason I believe _____ is _____. For example, ____ and _____. According to the text, _____. Based on what I read, _____. Finally, _____.

PARAGRAPH THREE:

The second reason I believe _____ is _____. For example, ____ and _____. According to the text, _____. Based on what I read, _____. Finally _____.

PARAGRAPH FOUR:

The third reason I believe _____ is _____. For example, ____ and _____. According to the text, _____. Based on what I read, _____. Finally, _____.

PARAGRAPH FIVE:

In conclusion, _____. I believe this because _____, _____, and _____. For this reason, _____.

SUMMARY

Target responses are essential when planning with the end in mind. Develop target responses across content areas to hold students accountable for self-assessment, self-monitoring, and grade-level achievement while also staying true to teacher clarity. When planning, start with the end result. Work backward to isolate the standards so you can create learning intentions that are specific to the target response you want your students to provide. Make sure to scaffold your target responses to reach all learners. This also provides a clear understanding of what's expected for students' final written response. See page 146 for a Target Response Template you can copy and use.

CHAPTER 8

ASSESSMENT AND DATA

What comes next, after the planning and teaching? Assessment drives instruction and, in this chapter, we'll look at different types of assessment that support teacher clarity, such as:

- Embedding self-assessment checks for students throughout a lesson

- Using formative assessment to drive instruction and create intervention models for reteaching or **extension** (challenging students who have met or have already exceeded the standard)

- Using assessments *for learning, as learning,* and *of learning*

As previously stated, assessment and data should drive instruction. If we're not analyzing our assessment data, then how do we know what students have learned and where they still need support?

Assessment data is not just for teachers, though. When you practice teacher clarity, you integrate students to be part of the assessment process. In all elements of learning, student-teacher communication is key!

Self-assessment helps students measure their own learning, empowering them to adjust their path toward mastery of the learning goal.

Self-assessment can be integrated into your classroom in many different ways. You can start small, with a few simple additions to your instructional day. I like to use the following methods in my own classroom:

1. Self-Assessment Tickets

2. Self-Assessment Turn-in Bins

3. Formative Assessment

4. For Learning, As Learning, Of Learning

SELF-ASSESSMENT TICKETS

Self-Assessment Tickets effectively and gradually implement self-assessment into your instructional day. With the help, support, and creativity of my principal, I was able to develop the following Self-Assessment Tickets when teaching 3rd grade in Southern California.

Self-Assessment Tickets help students assess their knowledge before and after learning a new concept. The tickets are easy to use, and students soon get used to the idea that they have to monitor their learning throughout the lesson.

To start, give each student a Self-Assessment Ticket before your lesson (see page 139 for a general Learning Objective template you can copy and use). As you open the lesson and state your learning intention, ask students to rate their understanding of the learning intention.

Name _____ Date _____

LEARNING OBJECTIVE

....

....

SELF-ASSESSMENT

	I totally understand and can teach my peers. (4)	I almost have it, but I may need a little more practice. (3)	I am a little confused and need some clarification. (2)	I am lost. Please reteach me. (1)
Before Lesson				
After Lesson				
Teacher Analysis				

POST-LESSON REFLECTION

- I feel ...
- I know ...
- My goal is ...
- I enjoyed ...
- I did not like ...

- I would like it if ...
- I need help with ...
- I am worried about ...
- Next, I would like to ...
- What I liked about this lesson was ...

....

....

....

....

I like to use these four levels of understanding (Marzano et al., 2017):

4. I totally understand and can teach my peers.

3. I almost have it, but I may need a little more practice.

2. I am a little confused and need some clarification.

1. I am lost. Please reteach me.

Students write a check mark in the box that most accurately describes their level of understanding prior to starting the lesson. You can also have students write down the learning objective during this time.

Once students write their check mark, ask them to place the ticket on the side of their table or desk. Remind them that they'll come back to it later. Then, start teaching your lesson.

Once you're done teaching, ask students to come back to their Self-Assessment Ticket and rate their level of understanding now that the lesson is over. I also like to include a reflection portion where students can write how they feel about their learning. Remind them that it is okay if their level of understanding did not improve or even went down. This is where valuable learning can take place. When students can address that they still have work to do in order to meet the learning intention, they enter the Learning Pit as discussed on page 34. When students recognize what they need to do to meet the goal or what they still need clarification on from the lesson, they are engaging in the learning process.

You can assign an independent practice for students to complete that matches the learning intention and skill students are self-assessing. When students are done completing the task, have them attach their Self-Assessment Ticket to their assignment.

I also include a teacher analysis on the ticket. This space is for my analysis as I check my students' work to see if their self-assessment aligns with what they were able to produce during independent practice.

Using Self-Assessment Tickets does take practice. Students need to feel comfortable being vulnerable and be able to admit that their level of understanding may be at a 1. When you first start using these tickets, students may not check off their true level of understanding in fear that others may see that they don't know something. But once you've communicated to your class that this ticket is meant for them to monitor their own progress, they'll be more comfortable with using the ticket correctly.

SELF-ASSESSMENT TURN-IN BINS

I created self-assessment turn-in bins, which are really easy to set up. I use four different bins labeled with each level of understanding:

4. I totally understand and can teach my peers.

3. I almost have it, but I may need a little more practice.

2. I am a little confused and need some clarification.

1. I am lost. Please reteach me.

Students then choose their level of understanding when turning in their work, whether it's an independent practice page or a quick assessment. This supports me as the classroom teacher in making sure that I understand my students' feelings about an assignment.

Set up the self-assessment turn-in bins so they're visible and easily accessible as students turn in their work.

Just like with the Self-Assessment Tickets, students need to feel comfortable when using this system. If you develop a classroom of trust and acceptance, students are more apt to use the turn-in bins correctly.

This system allows you to organize your students' work with more ease, as their intervention groups are already set up through the bins. Students who turn in their work into the bin that is marked with the level of understanding of 1 are more than likely going to need some academic interventions. Students whose work is in the level 4 bin may need some academic extension.

ASSESSMENT *FOR* LEARNING

The heart of assessment is seeing how students are learning. Students should practice and review concepts beyond cumulative or end-of-unit assessments. When they are spiraling through the standards and skills to gain more mastery and practice, formative assessment, or assessment for learning, comes into play. Formative assessment, when created collaboratively among grade-level teams, can drive instruction and help to create intervention opportunities for reteaching or extension.

Formative assessment is used not just to monitor each student's learning, but also to advance it. As explained in *Concise Answers to Frequently Asked Questions about Professional Learning Communities at Work*, formative assessment informs the student of their progress in becoming proficient while informing the teacher about the effectiveness of instruction and where to go next in the instructional process (DuFour et al., 92).

Formative assessments can also be as simple as the daily checks for understanding during instruction through the use of whiteboards, exit tickets, or independent practice.

- Whiteboards can be used during the gradual release of a direct instruction lesson. Students can write their thinking and answers on the whiteboard, which makes it feasible for you to check on them while standing in front of the entire class. Sheet protectors can also be used as whiteboards. Create sheets to put into the sheet protector that students may need for the lesson. For example, when teaching students about place value, ordering numbers, or comparing numbers, a sheet with a place value chart can be slid into the sheet protector, and students can use it to easily write their answers on and wipe their answers off.

- Exit tickets can be an effective way to check for your students' understanding at the end of the lesson. Format the tickets to ask a question or to have students practice a skill that was just taught. Exit tickets also give you the opportunity to challenge student thinking by asking higher-level or error-analysis questions.

- Independent practice should be used as formative assessment. Independent practice gives students the opportunity to practice a skill on their own. Using students' independent practice as a formative assessment also gives teachers the opportunity to assess skills in which students need support, or skills where students need to be challenged or have their thinking extended.

It is important for teams to come together and use **common formative assessments** to help guide instruction as a team.

Common formative assessments are created by collaborative teams and can help identify individual students who need additional time and support, provide students with targeted interventions, give students new opportunities to demonstrate their learning, and inform and improve their instruction by analyzing evidence of student learning.

As effective teachers, we're assessing our students' learning while we're teaching and checking for understanding. Here are some steps I have taken with my team to create common formative assessments:

- Isolate the standards for the particular upcoming unit you'll be teaching

- Create learning intentions for those isolated standards

- Use the learning intentions to create assessment questions

Common formative assessments work well as a pre- and post-test for your unit for students to see their growth and assess what they think they'll need more support in throughout the unit. They will also help your grade-level team see which students need more support and/or extension for particular skills, and will allow the team to see which areas need reteaching or extension. It's also a great way to compare data. Sometimes teachers use different strategies, and that's okay! Comparing information from different classes can help teachers collaborate on best practices and share what worked well for their students.

ASSESSMENT AS LEARNING

Assessment as learning means the student is the "critical connector" between assessment and their learning (Earl

2013, 43). According to Dr. Lorna M. Earl, retired associate professor from the Ontario Institute for Studies in Education at the University of Toronto, this happens when students personally monitor what they're learning. When the teacher gives them feedback, they can use the specific and effective feedback to adjust their learning and make sense of the learning objective they're trying to reach. You can support assessment as learning in the following ways:

- Encourage students to self-assess using levels of understanding as discussed earlier in this chapter.

- Using Self-Assessment Tickets during lessons for new concepts.

- Have students keep track of their own assessment data and reflect on their learning. For example, students can use their work and assessments to graph their scores.

- Have students compare their assessment scores over time and think about ways in which they can improve in the future. Seeing their progression using data tracking will also help students understand that learning is a progression.

- Have students develop their own goals for the school year. This can be over a short period of time. If students know what they want to accomplish as the end result, then they can set expectations for themselves to reach that goal. Along the way, they can focus on what they need to do to reach that goal and make progress.

ASSESSMENT *OF* LEARNING (SUMMATIVE ASSESSMENT)

Assessment of learning is the type of assessment that is most commonly used in schools (Earl 2013, 43). It's a communication tool that lets parents know their child's learning progress in school. Usually, assessment of learning is done at the end of the unit, and can come in the form of a test or exam.

Assessments of learning measure student achievement and determine if instructional goals have been met. This type of assessment has been widely accepted and is the most understood among teachers and parents; however, they aren't always the most fair or accurate (Earl, 44). Teachers across the same grade level weigh grades differently, assign different projects and assessments, and create grades that may be more subjective.

Additionally, an assessment of learning doesn't take a student's learning progression into consideration. If our grade-level standards spiral and the learning goals build on the previous year's standards, then a student's learning is continuous, meaning it builds on the foundation that was set in previous years. For example, in kindergarten, students learn to ask and answer questions about key details in a text. We build upon that standard in 1st grade, and by 2nd grade they are expected to ask and answer who, what, where, when, why, and how questions as well. We continue to build on learning goals in such a manner all the way until high school.

Although summative assessments are helpful, it is also important that students clearly know what will be assessed during that summative assessment. This way, students can track their own learning and know what is expected at the end of a unit.

SUMMARY

Assessment drives instruction. Assessment must also maintain components of teacher clarity to help students keep track of their own learning as well as take ownership of their learning goals. This includes providing students with clear examples, informing students of what is expected of them, explaining the purpose of the unit or lesson, and providing rubrics or other self-assessment.

We need different types of assessments to help guide our instruction and ensure that our students are learning. It is equally important to use these assessments to provide clarity to our students about their progress.

CHAPTER 9

COOPERATIVE LEARNING ACTIVITIES

Teaching isn't *all* about explicit instruction. It is also important to give students opportunities to put those skills into practice. One way to do this is through **cooperative learning activities**, or activities in which students work together to extend previously learned skills. This also makes the learning engaging and purposeful.

When assigning cooperative learning, I often combine several skills into one layered activity.

Here are some examples of cooperative learning activities:

- Jigsaw Method

- Reciprocal Teaching

- Reaching Consensus

- Collaborative Conversations

JIGSAW METHOD

The jigsaw classroom is a research-based cooperative learning technique invented and developed in the early 1970s by Elliot Aronson, an American psychologist. He conducted experiments on the theory of cognitive dissonance, the idea that when two actions or ideas are not psychologically consistent, people do all in their power to change them until they become consistent. Through his research and studies, he invented the Jigsaw Classroom, a cooperative teaching technique. "The jigsaw classroom has a four-decade track record of successfully reducing racial conflict and increasing positive educational outcomes such as improved test performance, reduced absenteeism, and greater liking for school" (Jigsaw.org 2020).

According to Jigsaw.org, the jigsaw method can be implemented by dividing your students into groups of five to six and designating one student as the leader. You would then divide the lesson or reading passage into five to six sections and assign each student to learn one section.

Give your students time to read over their section and become very familiar with it. After students have had time to read over their section, form groups of students by having one student from each group join other students assigned to the same section.

Bring the students back to their original groups and ask them to present their segment to their group. As students are completing these tasks, walk around the room, listen, and observe the process of students working together. At the end of this activity, use an exit ticket to assess student knowledge of the information they were learning. You can also assign a group activity that they need to complete together in their group, individually, or as a whole group.

RECIPROCAL TEACHING

Reciprocal teaching is a structured discussion and reading routine that consists of four strategies students take on while reading a piece of text:

SUMMARIZING

In this role, students will retell what they've read, learned, or completed in their own words. They will be prepared to share their ideas with their group, making sure that they have created a summary that their peers will understand. See page 147 for an expanded version of the following template to copy and hand out to students.

Name_____

SUMMARIZE

Identify key details and explain them in your own words.

The text is about _____ in this section.

First: _____

Next: _____

Then: _____

The big idea is _____

Important details are _____

_____

The author is trying to explain _____

_____

_____

QUESTIONING

As questioners, students will come up with questions about the topic their group has been assigned. There may be questions related to the reading that they want their group to answer, or there could be unanswered questions that they have about the topic that they'd like to present to their group. See page 148 for an expanded version of the following template to copy and hand out to students.

Name: _____

QUESTION

Ask questions as you read that are based on the text.

What is your opinion of _____ ?

What if _____ ?

Why is _____ so important?

What would happen if? _____

Why do you think? _____

How are _____ and _____ alike?

How are _____ and _____ different?

When / where is: _____

CLARIFYING

When clarifying, students will address confusing parts or bring up things that they feel may need clarification within their group. They will also work to clarify questions that their group partners may have while working together. See page 149 for an expanded version of the following template to copy and hand out to students.

Name: _____

CLARIFY

To clarify means to understand things more clearly.

Please explain the word. _____

_____

I need to reread because _____

I don't understand _____

I can make clearer by _____

I think this means _____ because

_____

A question I would like answered is _____

_____

_____

PREDICTING

In this role, students will make predictions based on the reading, or any other task their group is working on together. The student will lead the group in a conversation about their predictions and how they made those predictions. See page 150 for an expanded version of the following template to copy and hand out to students.

Name: _____   _____

PREDICT

Use clues from the text to think about what might happen next.

I think because _____

_____

Based on _____ , I _____

I predict _____

I think they will _____ because

_____

My prediction is _____ because

_____

I already know _____ , so I can predict

_____

The main idea of reciprocal teaching is to give students the strategies to make meaning, practice self-questioning, and chunk text into smaller passages. Students are taught to pause after reading smaller chunks of text and discuss the reading using these four strategies (Fisher et al. 2016, 98).

In my classroom, I teach each of the four strategies explicitly before having students begin these tasks as a group. Once they have had practice in using the strategies, I assign groups and make sure each person has a role.

We usually read the text as a whole group, making sure to chunk each section as we're reading so students have an opportunity to complete the task that is assigned to their role.

These strategies help support teacher clarity because students have the ability to use the strategies independently while knowing what is expected of each role and its outcome. Teachers are able to employ reciprocal teaching almost immediately because students inherently take on the roles and practice the strategies while reading a text (Fisher et al., 99).

REACHING CONSENSUS

Teaching students to come to a consensus while working in groups helps build a foundation for them to collaborate as they enter high grade levels and eventually join the workforce. Students will also be able to practice targeted skills while showing independence and problem solving in a group.

There are various ways to set up your groups. Assigning roles for each student in the group demonstrates teacher clarity and helps students reach a consensus. Potential roles include the following:

QUESTIONER

The Questioner makes sure their teammates can make sense of the problem. They help their team identify what they know about the problem and what they need to find out. Some questions to help the Questioner while meeting with their group are:

- Did we all get the same answer?

- Do our answers make sense?

- Can we solve this in different ways?

See page 151 for a Questioner checklist you can copy and hand out to your groups.

RECORDER

The Recorder records their teammates' questions, ideas, or misunderstandings. They use pictures or words to explain their team's thinking. These questions will guide the Recorder as they help their group:

- Did you double-check your work?

- Can you explain how you solved the problem?

- Is there another way our team can solve this?

See page 151 for a Recorder checklist you can copy and hand out to your groups.

MANAGER

The Manager accesses help from the teacher or another group when the entire group is stuck, and then they'll share the answer with the group. Some questions the Manager can ask their group are:

- Who can explain what we have done so far?

- Where are we stuck?

- What other information do we need?

- Does this answer make sense to everyone?

See page 152 for a Manager checklist you can copy and hand out to your groups.

DIRECTOR

The Director keeps team members on task and helps to answer questions. They also help to keep track of the time while making sure everyone participates. Some questions they may ask their group are:

- Who has another idea?

- Do you have any questions about our work?

- Does anyone agree or disagree?

These roles and expectations will ensure students work together in a calm and cohesive way.

See page 152 for a Director checklist you can copy and hand out to your groups.

Before assigning these roles and having student groups begin on their own, take some time to teach the concept as a whole group. In my classroom, I like to introduce this lesson by relating it to families and friends trying to pick what they're going to eat for dinner. Sometimes it's a long conversation with lots of disagreements, and that's okay!

Here is a sample lesson you can use to teach students how to reach a consensus in a group:

Standard	*CCSS.ELA-LITERACY.SL.3.1.B* *Follow agreed-upon rules for discussions (e.g., gaining the floor in respectful ways, listening to others with care, speaking one at a time about the topics and texts under discussion).*
Hook (Make Connections)	• *Talk about an instance when you tried to come to a consensus with friends and family. I like to use the example of trying to decide what we want to eat for dinner as a family.*

Learning Intention	• We are learning how to come to a consensus (come to an agreement) when working together in a group.
Review (Prior Skills)	• An agreement is when you think the same thing as someone else. • A disagreement is when you do not think the same thing as someone else. • When you justify something, you're proving that you are right with evidence.

Big Idea (Why)	**Success Criteria**
	• *I can use academic language to communicate my ideas when working in a group.*
	• *I can explain my thinking in a respectful way.*
	• *I can use SLANT when listening to others in a group setting.*
	    SLANT:
	    S: Sit up tall
	    L: Lean in and listen
	    A: Ask and answer questions
	    N: Nod for understanding
	    T: Talk to students and teachers
	
	Real-World Connection
	• *We come to consensus daily. We talk about what we want to play at recess, what we want to eat for dinner with our families, or what we want to watch on TV. Think about times when you and your friends or family have had to come to consensus.*
	• *Reaching consensus is coming together as scholars to discuss ideas and answers.*
	• *Your goal is to come to a consensus, or an agreement about what you think.*
	• *You can always respectfully disagree, but make sure you have evidence to justify your answer.*
	• *Collaborators are people who work together.*
	• *Consensus is coming to an agreement.*

Model (Skills, Concepts, Metacognition)	1. Lead Speaker will share their answer and how they got it. 2. Lead Speaker will ask if anyone agrees or disagrees. 3. Collaborators will share their agreements or disagreements. 4. Finally, collaborators will share other ways of finding the answer. Questions and Frames to Use: • Do you agree with my answer? • Can you think of another way to solve it? • Yes, I agree because ___. • No, I respectfully disagree because ___. • Another way you can solve this is ___.
Guided Practice	• Show one problem to students that the whole class needs to solve. Hold a whole-group discussion using the format from the model to explain and fish bowl, or demonstrate for all to see, what reaching consensus looks like before students try in their own groups.
Closure	1. What was our learning objective? 2. What happens when we don't reach a consensus? 3. Is it okay to disagree with our teammates?
Independent Practice	• Provide students with one math question that they need to answer independently, and then assign the roles for groups to try reaching consensus on their own.

COLLABORATIVE CONVERSATIONS

Giving students an opportunity to talk with one another about what they're learning helps them gain a better understanding.

MUSIC ROTATIONS

Get your students moving with this sharing strategy. When you have taught content and you are ready for your students to share what they've learned, have them pair up with other students through music. Tell your students you're going to play music, and that when the music is playing they will walk around the room. They will walk across from where they're sitting, and as they are walking they need to fill the space of the room. When the music stops, they will stop moving and partner up with the person nearest to them. They will then share their knowledge with their partner.

NUMBERED HEADS

Group your students in groups of four. Number each student in the group one through four. Give each group of students a task or question to answer. Tell them to be prepared to share their answers with the whole class. Give the group time to discuss and come to a consensus about their answer. When all groups are ready, call a number one through four. The person from each group who was assigned that number will share their group's answer with the whole class.

TALKING CHIPS

Talking chips are little counters that are used to help student groups facilitate their conversations. You can use tokens from a board game, mini erasers, or even pieces of cut-up paper.

Students hold on to their chips, and during their group conversations, they can use their chips to talk. Each chip they have can be used to contribute to the group. Once their chips are all used, then they cannot share with their group anymore until everyone has used their talking chips. You can pass out more tokens as needed as groups finish their conversations.

In this structured language routine, students use a talking stick to take turns sharing. You can use Popsicle sticks, decorated nail files, or anything creative that your students can hold. I printed out my Bitmoji and put it on popsicle sticks. My students use these as their talking sticks. When a student is holding their talking stick, that means it is their turn to share with the group. When they're done, they pass the stick to someone else for 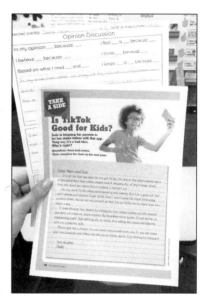 their turn to share. When choosing the first person to use the talking stick in the group, I will usually say something like, "The person wearing the most yellow in the group can start with the talking stick first."

STRUCTURED LANGUAGE FRAMES

Structured language frames support students with their collaborative conversations based on the function of the language that you want your students to practice. For example, in this opinion discussion, students used opinion frames to discuss their perspective about TikTok. They used opinion language frames to discuss their own differences in opinion using details from the article to support their thinking.

These strategies can be used across the disciplines, making collaboration and structured conversations a versatile learning strategy. Making sure to integrate structured language into your daily routines is so beneficial for students. It helps them understand the learning objectives more clearly, promotes collaboration, and gives them the opportunity to express their learning verbally.

SUMMARY

When students can take skills that they have explicitly learned and practice them as a layered activity with other students, it helps to deepen their learning and their understanding. Using cooperative learning activities will require classroom teachers to set expectations, set clear learning goals, and make sure students are prepared to practice several skills in one activity.

CHAPTER 10

SUCCESS IN DISTANCE LEARNING

In 2020, a shift to distance learning and **hybrid models** (in person and distance learning combined) transformed teaching strategies and learning modules. As teachers, we were forced to adapt to a new style of teaching, assessment, progress monitoring, and developing and maintaining student-teacher relationships. But as teachers, we are rising to the occasion to provide our students with quality instruction, support, and the same family environment we all strive to create in our classrooms.

One question I had when I started distance learning in March of 2020 was, "How can I continue to have teacher clarity while teaching online?" As I continuously work to answer this question for myself, I've come up with a few tips and ideas to continue to practice teacher clarity in the classroom during distance learning and while I am teaching in person with social distancing.

TAKE CARE OF YOURSELF

First and foremost, the most important thing is to take care of yourself. As the old adage goes, you can't pour from an empty cup. You need to make the time to take care of yourself and do the things that give you energy, bring you peace, and make you happy. While I was teaching during distance learning when schools were first shut down, it was hard to separate school life from home life. As a teacher and a mom, it had already been a struggle to turn off teacher mode and enter into mom mode once I got home. But when you add in teaching from home, the line just blurred.

I realized that I needed to set some boundaries for myself. I made a schedule to help organize the time I needed to spend online while teaching and the time I needed to spend grading. I also made dedicated office hours for students and parents to reach me instantly.

In creating my schedule, I also carved out time for my home life. I made sure to make a lot of time for my two boys when I was not distracted by my phone, computer, or school work. Within that schedule, I also started incorporating opportunities for me to enjoy things that made me happy, like going to the gym, getting my nails done, or visiting with friends. Sometimes, it is important to separate yourself from the work because you don't want to let it consume you.

CONNECT WITH STUDENTS

When our schools first closed for distance learning, I was able to gain a lot of experience teaching. Since I had already created strong relationships with my students, this made it easy to continue to connect with them online being that they already knew who I was and what I expected. In turn, knowing who my students were, what they were capable of completing, and how they learned best also made it easier.

Starting with distance learning from the get-go can make developing and maintaining those positive student-teacher relationships difficult; however, it can be done. Make time to participate in online, getting-to-know-you activities through virtual meeting places.

USE CLARITY TO EXPLAIN EXPECTATIONS

Teacher clarity can come in the form of clear behavioral expectations, not just academic expectations. Whether you are distance learning, hybrid learning, or in-person learning with social distancing, setting clear behavioral expectations is extremely important. Students need to know what you expect of them and how you'll support them to meet those expectations. This will help build strong teacher-student relationships because students will know that you care about their well-being and behavior, in addition to their academic success.

DISTANCE LEARNING

For distance learning, set expectations for how assignments should be completed, when they are expected to be turned into you for a grade, how to access assignments on the platform your classroom is using, and behavior during live meetings. You can even keep a digital folder with a list of these expectations for you and your students to refer to as you review them.

Before you start a live virtual meeting with your students, review your behavioral expectations to set the stage for your students.

As previously mentioned, direct instruction provides teacher clarity because it involves clear modeling and an appropriate gradual release for students to practice new skills. If you're teaching online, direct instruction benefits students greatly because it provides specific steps and clarity on how to reach learning goals. Offer your students opportunities to work collaboratively after learning new skills through direct instruction. You can create groups through your online learning platform or use video-recording platforms to encourage students to collaborate through digital interfaces. While doing this, set up expectations for behavior as well as for their group projects and assignments. You can still give students success criteria and support them with teacher clarity by giving them strong examples, preparing them through direct instruction, and modeling through your own example videos and online resources.

STUDENT SOCIAL AND EMOTIONAL LEARNING

Adjusting to this new format of learning is as difficult for kids as it is for adults. Students may be missing an emotional and social connection if they're not attending school in person. Make sure to check in with them to see how they're doing socially and emotionally. A digital check-in form can assess students' emotional and social well-being, helping you to determine which students may need more support or a one-on-one check-in via a digital meeting platform.

IN-PERSON LEARNING

If you're teaching in person and socially distancing, review expectations and model the appropriate social distancing procedures for your students. Consistently recognize students who are following those expectations by rewarding them with your schoolwide rewards, classroom incentives, or other positive behavioral incentives in place in your classroom.

Depending on your school and district's COVID-19 protocols, you can also take your students outside or into a larger environment, like a gym or cafeteria, to practice classroom circles. After modeling the expectations during classroom circles, use that opportunity to create relationships, have fun, and bring some normalcy to your class family.

For the same reasons, direct instruction can also be beneficial during in-person learning while practicing social distancing. You would need to adjust the way your students are partner sharing or working on collaborative activities when practicing the new skills they're learning. One way to do this is to create student cohorts that can work with each other during cooperative activities as they spend time together in their rows, while sitting together at lunch, or during their "specials" time. (Specials time consists of the 35-minute to 1-hour block for classes like music, PE, library, or computers.) If your school and district allow it, you can also have students complete cooperative activities in a larger environment like a gym or outside.

STUDENT SOCIAL AND EMOTIONAL LEARNING

If you're teaching in person while social distancing, give students the opportunity to check in with you, your school counselor, or other adults on campus. You can use a check-in sheet like this to help you better understand your students' emotional needs:

Name: _____ Date: _____

DAILY CHECK-IN

I am grateful for: _____
_____

What makes me happy is: _____
_____

TODAY I FEEL...

Happy	Excited	Anxious	Scared	Frustrated	Bored
Sad	Tired	Nervous	Mad	Focused	Calm

Circle the emotion that matches your feelings today.

If you feel comfortable, you can explain more about your feelings on the lines below.

_____
_____
_____
_____

See page 153 for a Daily Check-In sheet that you can copy and use.

KEEP A POSITIVE TEACHER MINDSET

We have all experienced difficult situations in teaching, and we may all agree that teaching during a pandemic has probably been one of the most trying times of our teaching career. Looking back on your experiences though, can you think of another difficult situation you've encountered? We have all had those moments when we may have questioned our "why."

Were you able to change your words in those moments to help change your teacher mindset?

Sometimes, that may be hard to do. But remember, you are actively sculpting each student's brain in class (online or in person) every day!

Research has shown that school experiences with above-average teachers can raise student achievement in mathematics by as much as 95 percent (Ferguson 1998, 18). According to brain researcher Eric Jensen (Jensen 2017, 72–73), differences in academic performance among students usually involve three neurocognitive systems:

1. Language. Students from lower socioeconomic areas do not have as much exposure to language or language skills during their early years (up to 18 months). This may contribute to reading difficulties in school-age children.

2. Memory. According to research, students from low socioeconomic areas develop baseline working memory far more slowly than their peers in more affluent areas.

3. Cognitive Control. This is the power to nimbly switch gears and adjust to transitions. Poorer students struggle with transitions more than nonpoor students.

These differences can reduce school performance and are commonly found in lower socioeconomic classes, but there is good news! Strong teaching, positive teacher-student relationships, and mindset can change this.

We can start by changing expectations for our students. Teachers all over the country are setting high expectations for all of their students, not just the ones who are already achieving.

Great teachers set a tone and create an atmosphere of genuine affection and concern, helping their students flourish in their growth and enrichment mindsets.

Carol Dweck, author of *Growth Mindset: The New Psychology of Success* and a pioneering researcher of growth mindset, says, "When teachers are judging them, students will sabotage the teacher by not trying. But when students understand that school is a way for them to grow their minds—they do not insist on sabotaging themselves."

As teachers, we have the ability to help shape our students' mindsets. By creating a positive learning environment, we can mold them to positively contribute to their own achievement. "Whenever students feel better emotionally, good things happen" (Jensen 2017, 14).

So how can we make our students feel better emotionally during these unprecedented times to help them achieve more academically?

Jensen explains that there are two neurotransmitters associated with improved affect: dopamine and serotonin.

Higher dopamine levels create greater learning, greater working memory, greater cognitive flexibility, and greater effort (Jensen 2016, 19). You can increase your students' dopamine production with gross motor activities, novelties, surprising and fun activities, and anticipation of rewarding events.

Higher serotonin levels contribute to better attention, learning, mood regulation, and long-term memory (Jensen 2016, 19). You can increase your student's serotonin production by increasing calmness, feelings of control, the use of predictable routines, cooperation, and camaraderie among classmates and your class family. For example, provide students time to practice mindfulness activities during the school day. You and your students can practice relaxing breathing patterns, meditation, or journaling to help promote calmness.

According to Jensen, noradrenaline is also a powerful neuro-transmitter that can foster better focus and long-term memory. High levels of urgency, excitement, and perception of risk stimulate noradrenaline. When students present in front of their peers they feel all those things. This helps students focus and recenter.

When your students present in front of their peers under a deadline, they feel urgency and excitement, and they are taking risks. You can provide students with opportunities to do these types of activities, or fast energizers, online or in person to help boost those levels of neurotransmitters in their brains.

As teachers, we can set the stage for our students. We have the ability to create a positive environment where they feel welcome, supported, appreciated, and garner a sense of reciprocated respect. We can influence our students' behavior for the better.

Here are some more examples of how we can boost positivity as well as levels of noradrenaline, dopamine, and serotonin in our classrooms, both online and in person:

- Model Optimism

- Set Expectations

- Conduct Classroom Circles

- Reward Consistently and Fairly

MODEL OPTIMISM

Being optimistic or positive means that you hold the mindset that negative events are temporary and manageable. You can model this optimism with your students daily.

Greet your students at the door with your smile, your positive energy, and your personable hellos. Take the time to notice your students' fresh haircuts or new shoes, or look closely to see if they have something on their mind.

Set the standard high each day and show them that you're happy to be there and be their teacher. You can do that by simply modeling positive talk, a calm voice, and a personality that shows you care about them as people as much as you care about their academic success.

SET EXPECTATIONS

Make sure students know what's expected of them online or while teaching in person. Make a list of specific behavioral expectations. Keep them succinct, positive, and attainable. As mentioned previously, it is important to review them daily, weekly, and monthly. It would benefit students to see them posted online in your classroom stream, or hanging in your classroom for students to refer to and be reminded of daily.

CONDUCT CLASSROOM CIRCLES

Check-in circles are a great way to start the day, whether you're online or in person.

During a check-in circle, students are invited to share their feelings and listen to others. Have the student stand or hold a talking stick or other item to make sure that only one person is talking at a time. You can also conduct these circles online through an online meeting platform. Don't forget that students can opt out if they choose, but hopefully they'll gain enough confidence to come back and join the next time.

Build comfort and trust with simple activities during the check-in circle. Here are a few examples:

1. Ask each student to rate how they are feeling on a scale of 1 to 5. You can start the activity by sharing what you are feeling and why.

2. Play the game You're in My Boat, when students take turns sharing something about themselves or an experience they have had recently. They might say something like, "I really love hamburgers," or "I was mad at my mom this morning." Students who agree with the statements can get up and change seats or raise their hands. You can choose to discuss these things with the circle, too.

3. Peacemaking circles can be used to resolve conflicts between students. Encourage students to reach out to you if they have problems. You can create whole class circles, or create circles that are made up of the students involved in a certain situation. Define the issue and raise awareness of each student's feelings and perspectives. Make sure to also have students share a positive thought about the student(s) they are in conflict with.

REWARD CONSISTENTLY AND FAIRLY

Rewarding students with prizes, points, and free recesses will definitely get students to buy into what you're doing and elicit positive behaviors from students, thus helping your classroom management.

However, the true rewards come from *your* positivity. Here are a list of ways to reward your students:

- Offer a thank you, eye contact, and a smile when they raise their hands to speak. Acknowledge students when they meet behavioral expectations.

- Greet them at the door each morning with a smile and a "Good morning!"

- Surprise them with "lunch with the teacher" passes, or with positive praise when they have put quality effort into assignments or assessments.

Students love the feeling of being recognized. Always take a moment to notice and recognize the good.

SUMMARY

As teachers, we've learned new ways to teach, engage our students, and be mindful of their circumstances as we shifted to distance learning. It's important that through this new journey in education we take care of our own well-being, as well as take time to connect with students. Social emotional learning and keeping a positive teacher mindset is, and always will be, extremely important. We have the opportunity to model optimism and help support our students in ways we never before thought were possible.

CONCLUSION

What happens after you've put teacher clarity into place in your classroom, in your instruction, and with your students?

Celebrate your successes, as well as your students' successes. I think teachers are their own worst critics. We need to stop that.

Take a look around and admire what you've already accomplished. Think about the time and energy you've spent making sure you're doing what's best for your students. Celebrate your successes as a teacher, as a professional. You've done so much!

Maybe you met your first goal toward having teacher clarity. Maybe you got your grade-level team on board to help develop a path toward backward unit planning. Whatever progress you have made, celebrate it! Take time at the end of the day to think about the positive parts. Write them down or send yourself an email about it. Reflect on the good.

The same goes for your students. Since we're with them day in and day out, it's sometimes hard to see the changes and progress they've made that's right in front of our eyes. Take some time to reflect *with* your students. Celebrate their successes together, and honor their hard work and commitment. Ultimately, you were the force that brought them there through teacher clarity. You helped sparked that change, that progression toward mastery.

You've got this!

GLOSSARY

Assessment as learning: Assessment that is done by the student on his or her own learning.

Assessment for learning: Assessment that is done to see how students are learning and how to move forward with instruction.

Assessment of learning: Assessment that is done at the end of the unit and can come in the form of a test or exam.

Backward mapping: The idea of planning with the end in mind when thinking about a unit plan or lesson plan.

Big idea: The portion of the lesson where the teacher makes a real-world connection to the skill or learning intention that students are tasked to meet.

Closure: The end of the lesson, when the students are asked questions to ensure their understanding of the learning intention.

Collaboration: Teachers working together to improve instruction, learning, and assessment for all students.

Collective teacher efficacy: Teachers working together in collaboration for the advancement of their students.

Common formative assessment: Formative assessments that are created by and used among grade-level teams in order to gather data that will help form instruction.

Cooperative learning activities: Learning activities in which students work together in a group, sharing responsibilities and taking ownership of their own learning.

Declarative lesson: A lesson in which students need to know or understand a concept.

Deconstructing standards: Taking about the content standards to determine specific learning intentions that will develop into lessons and unit plans.

Depth of knowledge: Questions designed to help students think more deeply about what they're learning and how they're applying their knowledge.

Effect size: Method for comparing results between groups.

Explicit comprehension: Understanding information from a text that is explicitly explained in the text.

Explicit instruction: A teaching strategy where the teacher clearly and explicitly explains the learning intention, clearly models the skill, guides students into practice while checking for understanding, and then closes the lesson with higher-level questioning.

Extrinsic motivation: Motivation that is created by external forces.

Feedback: Constructive and effective suggestions to help students meet learning goals.

Formative assessment: See "assessment for learning."

Growth mindset: Setting your mind to believe that effort is the path toward mastery; believing in the power of "yet."

Guided practice (gradual release): The part of the lesson where students are asked to practice the skill that is being taught and are given less and less support from the teacher until they're independently completing the skill.

Hook: The beginning of the lesson that "hooks" the learner into the lesson before even starting; it usually starts with an engaging story, question, or quick anecdote.

Independent practice: The practice of students completing tasks independently to assert their knowledge and independence in completing the learned skill.

Inferential comprehension: Using text details and personal experiences to make guesses and inferences about what the text is trying to explain.

Intentionality: Being purposeful and explicit in your teaching, planning, and assessment.

Intrinsic motivation: Motivation that is created internally, by one's own desire.

Jigsaw method: A cooperative teaching technique that can be implemented by dividing students into groups of five to six and designating one student as the leader.

Learning intentions (learning goal, learning objective): Goals for learning set forth by teachers based on content standards; made for students to understand and assess.

Learning Pit: The idea that when students talk about their own learning, it helps them to understand the progress they are making.

Levels of understanding: Levels for students to rate their understanding of a learning intention:

- 1 - I am lost. Please reteach me.
- 2 - I am a little confused and need some clarification.
- 3 - I almost have it, but I may need a little more practice.
- 4 - I totally understand and can teach my peers.

Modeling: The portion of the lesson where the teacher explicitly models the skill in order for students to understand how to complete it.

Procedural lesson: A lesson in which students need to do something.

Professional learning community: Working collaboratively in an ongoing process to achieve better results for students.

Progression of learning: The progress students make toward a learning goal or learning intention.

Reaching consensus: Coming to a respectful agreement as a group.

Reciprocal teaching: A structured discussion and reading routine that consists of strategies students use while reading a piece of text.

Review: The portion of the lesson where the teacher reviews previously learned skills to help the students make connections between what they've already learned and the new skill they're about to learn.

Self-assessment: Students taking ownership of their own learning and being able to assess their understanding of the learning intention.

Structured language frames: Language frames used to support students in the English language domains while they are speaking and writing.

Success criteria: "Specific, concrete, measurable statements that describe what success looks like when the learning goal is reached" (Hattie et al. 2017, 29).

Target response: A written response that is written to hit the grade-level target that is created by the teacher to support students in their writing.

Teacher clarity: A culture of teaching and collaboration that develops into a mindset that makes teaching streamlined and purposeful.

Think-pair-share: A form of student collaboration where students first think about a question, pair up with a partner, and then share their ideas; this is also an effective way to informally assess students.

APPENDIX

Name _____ Date _____

LEARNING OBJECTIVE

_____

_____

SELF-ASSESSMENT

	I totally understand and can teach my peers. (4)	I almost have it, but I may need a little more practice. (3)	I am a little confused and need some clarification. (2)	I am lost. Please reteach me. (1)
Before Lesson				
After Lesson				
Teacher Analysis				

REFLECTION

- I feel ...
- I know ...
- My goal is ...
- I enjoyed ...
- I did not like ...
- I would like it if ...
- I need help with ...
- I am worried about ...
- Next, I would like to ...
- What I liked about this lesson was ...

UNDERSTANDING

_____

_____

_____

_____

Name_____ Date_____

LEARNING OBJECTIVE

_____

_____

SELF-ASSESSMENT

	I totally understand and can teach my peers. (4)	I almost have it, but I may need a little more practice. (3)	I am a little confused and need some clarification. (2)	I am lost. Please reteach me. (1)
Before Lesson				
After Lesson				
Teacher Analysis				

POST-LESSON REFLECTION

- I feel …
- I know …
- My goal is …
- I enjoyed …
- I did not like …

- I would like it if …
- I need help with …
- I am worried about …
- Next, I would like to …
- What I liked about this lesson was …

_____

_____

_____

_____

_____

_____

© Marine Freibrun

GROWTH-MINDSET EXIT TICKET

Inspiration
I used today:

_____
_____
_____
_____
_____
_____

Perseverance
helped me today:

_____
_____
_____
_____
_____
_____

Challenges
I embraced
today:

_____
_____
_____
_____
_____
_____

POWERFUL WORDS!

THINK POSITIVELY!

1. _____   6. _____

2. _____   7. _____

3. _____   8. _____

4. _____   9. _____

5. _____   10. _____

WHAT HAPPENED THAT WAS GREAT?!

_____

_____

_____

_____

_____

WHAT MISTAKES DID YOU MAKE?

_____

_____

_____

POSITIVE WORD FOR THE DAY

_____

_____

DECONSTRUCTING STANDARDS TEMPLATE

STANDARD:

Sentence from Standard:	
Key Words and Phrases	
Actions and Verbs	
Learning Intention	
Sentence from Standard:	
Key Words and Phrases	
Actions and Verbs	
Learning Intention	
Sentence from Standard:	
Key Words and Phrases	
Actions and Verbs	
Learning Intention	

© Marine Freibrun

EXPLICIT INSTRUCTION
LESSON PLAN TEMPLATE

Standard	
Hook (Make Connections)	
Learning Intention	
Review (Prior Skills)	
Big Idea (Why)	
Model (Skills, Concepts, Metacognition)	
Guided Practice	
Closure	
Independent Practice	

© Marine Freibrun

SUCCESS CRITERIA

DESCRIBE CHARACTERS

- ☐ I can determine a character's feelings.
- ☐ I can determine a character's actions.
- ☐ I can determine a character's motivations.
- ☐ I can determine a character's traits.
- ☐ I can describe characters.
- ☐ I can use details from the text to support my thinking.
- ☐ I can cite evidence from the text to support my ideas.

SUCCESS CRITERIA

SUPPRORTING THE MAIN IDEA

- ☐ I determined the main idea.
- ☐ I cited enough evidence from the text to support the main idea.
- ☐ I included specific examples from the text.
- ☐ I used what does the text say starters in my response.
- ☐ My answer uses evidence from the text and it is clearly explained.

SUCCESS CRITERIA

COMPARE & CONTRAST

- ☐ I can explain how two texts are alike (compare).
- ☐ I can explain how two texts are different (contrast).
- ☐ I can use details from the text to support my ideas.
- ☐ I can cite evidence to support my ideas.
- ☐ I can use "what does the text say" starters to cite evidence.
- ☐ I can use compare and contrast signal words throughout my writing.

SUCCESS CRITERIA

OPINION WRITING

- ☐ I can support my opinion with reasons.
- ☐ I can support my opinion with examples.
- ☐ I can use details from different texts to support my opinion.
- ☐ I can use details from my personal experiences to support my opinion.
- ☐ I can cite evidence from different texts using "What does the text say?" starters.
- ☐ I can use opinion writing signal words.

© Marine Freibrun

SUCCESS CRITERIA

RECOUNTING

- [ ] I can write details about the beginning.
- [ ] I can write details about the middle.
- [ ] I can write details about the end.
- [ ] I can write details in the correct sequence of events.
- [ ] I can write complete sentences with subject and verb agreement.

SUCCESS CRITERIA

CENTRAL MESSAGE

- [ ] I can determine the message or theme of the story.
- [ ] I can support my ideals with details from the text.
- [ ] I can cite evidence to support my ideas.
- [ ] I can use the sequence of events to explain the central message.

SUCCESS CRITERIA

COMPARE & CONTRAST

- [ ] I can explain how two texts are alike (compare).
- [ ] I can explain how two texts are different (contrast).
- [ ] I can use details from the text to support my ideas.
- [ ] I can cite evidence to support my ideas.

SUCCESS CRITERIA

MAIN IDEA

- [ ] I can determine what the text is about (main idea).
- [ ] I can use details from the text to support the main idea.
- [ ] I can write details in the correct sequence of events.

© Marine Freibrun

TARGET RESPONSE TEMPLATE

Target Response	
Skills Students Need to Know	

Standards	
Learning Intentions	

Sentence Frames	

© Marine Freibrun

Name: _____

SUMMARIZE

Identify key details and explain them in your own words.

The text is about _____ in this section.

First: _____

_____

Next: _____

_____

Then: _____

_____

The big idea is _____

_____

_____

Important details are _____

_____

_____

_____

_____

The author is trying to explain _____

_____

_____

_____

_____

_____

_____

Name: _____

QUESTION

Ask questions as you read that are based on the text.

What is your opinion of _____ ?

_____

_____

What if _____ ?

Why is _____ so important?

_____

_____

What would happen if? _____

_____

_____

Why do you think? _____

_____

_____

How are _____ and _____ alike?

How are _____ and _____ different?

_____

_____

_____

_____

When / where is: _____

_____

_____

_____

_____

Name: _____

CLARIFY

To clarify means to understand things more clearly.

Please explain the word. _____

_____

_____

I need to reread because _____

_____

_____

I don't understand _____

_____

_____

I can make clearer by _____

_____

_____

I think this means _____ because

_____

_____

A question I would like answered is _____

_____

_____

_____

_____

_____

_____

Name: _____

PREDICT

Use clues from the text to think about what might happen next.

I think _____ because _____

_____

_____

_____

Based on _____ , I _____

_____

_____

_____

I predict _____

_____

_____

_____

I think they will _____ because

_____

_____

_____

My prediction is _____ because

_____

_____

I already know _____ , so I can predict

_____

_____

_____

_____

QUESTIONER

- Work with the group to make sure everyone understands the task and the solution plan and can explain whether the answer makes sense.

QUESTIONS TO ASK YOUR GROUP

☐ What do we know/need to know?

☐ What Is our plan?

☐ Does our answer mere sense?

RECORDER

- Show the thinking of the group that leads to the solution.
- Draw a picture.
- Write an equation.

QUESTIONS TO ASK YOUR GROUP

☐ Is this chart correct?

☐ Is this what you mean?

☐ How could we show this another way?

MANAGER

- Access help from the teacher or another group when the entire group Is stuck and then share the answer with the group.

QUESTIONS TO ASK YOUR GROUP

☐ Who can explain what we have done so far?

☐ Where are we stuck?

☐ What other information do we need?

☐ Does this answer make sense to everyone?

DIRECTOR

- Read the task/problem/assignment.
- Make sure all group members are on task and are participating.
- Watch the time.

QUESTIONS TO ASK YOUR GROUP

☐ Who has another idea?

☐ Do you have any questions about our work?

☐ Does anyone agree or disagree?

© Marine Freibrun

Name: _____ Date: _____

DAILY CHECK-IN

I am grateful for: _____
_____

What makes me happy is: _____
_____

TODAY I FEEL...

Happy	*Excited*	*Anxious*	*Scared*	*Frustrated*	*Bored*
Sad	*Tired*	*Nervous*	*Mad*	*Focused*	*Calm*

Circle the emotion that matches your feelings today.

If you feel comfortable, you can explain more about your feelings on the lines below.

_____
_____
_____
_____
_____
_____
_____
_____
_____
_____
_____
_____

REFERENCES

Almarode, John, Douglas Fisher, Kateri Thunder, John Hattie, and Nancy Frey. *Teaching Mathematics in the Visible Learning Classroom, Grades K–2*. Thousand Oaks, CA: Corwin Press, 2019.

DuFour, Richard, Rebecca DuFour, Mike Mattos, Robert Eaker, and Thomas Many. *Learning by Doing: A Handbook for Professional Learning Communities at Work*. Bloomington, IN: Solution Tree Press, 2016.

DuFour, Richard, Rebecca DuFour, Mike Mattos, Robert Eaker, and Thomas Many. *Concise Answers to Frequently Asked Questions about Professional Learning Communities at Work*. Bloomington, IN: Solution Tree Press, 2016.

Earl, Lorna. *Assessment as Learning: Using Classroom Assessment to Maximize Student Learning*. Thousand Oaks, CA: Corwin Press, 2013.

Ferguson, R. F. "Can Schools Narrow the Black-White Test Score Gap?" In C. Jencks and M. Phillips (Eds) *The Black-White Test Score Gap* (318–74). Washington, DC: Brookings Institution Press, 1998.

Fisher, Douglas, Nancy Frey, Olivia Amador, and Joseph Assof. *The Teacher Clarity Playbook, Grades K–12: A Hands-On Guide to Creating Learning Intentions and Success Criteria for Organized, Effective Instruction*. Thousand Oaks, CA: Corwin Press, 2018.

Hattie, John. *Visible Learning for Teachers: Maximizing Impact on Learning*. New York: Routledge, 2012.

Hattie, John, Douglas Fisher, Nancy Frey, Linda M. Gojak, Sara Delano Moore, and William Mellman. *Visible Learning for Mathematics, Grades K–12: What Works Best to Optimize Student Learning*. Thousand Oaks, CA: Corwin Press, 2016.

Hattie, John, and Klaus Zierer. *10 Mindframes for Visible Learning: Teaching for Success*. New York: Routledge, 2018.

Jensen, Eric. *Poor Students, Richer Teaching: Mindsets for Change (Data-Driven Strategies for Overcoming Student Poverty and Adversity in the Classroom to Increase Student Success)*. Bloomington, IN: Solution Tree Press, 2017.

The Jigsaw Classroom. n.d. "The Jigsaw Classroom." Accessed January 11, 2021. https://www.jigsaw.org.

Marzano, Robert, Jennifer Norford, Michelle Finn, and Douglas Finn III. *A Handbook for Personalized Competency-Based Education*. Bloomington, IN: Marzano Research, 2017.

Nottingham, Jill, James Nottingham, Mark Bollom, Joanne Nugent, and Lorna Pringle. *Learning Challenge Lessons, Elementary: 20 Lessons to Guide Young Learners through the Learning Pit*. Thousand Oaks, CA: Corwin Press, 2018.

TESS Consulting. n.d. "TESS Consulting Group, Training and Coaching for Focused Instruction." Accessed January 11, 2021. https://www.tesscg.com.

Wikimedia Foundation. "Madeline Cheek Hunter–Wikipedia." July 13, 2005. https://en.wikipedia.org/wiki/Madeline_Cheek_Hunter.

ACKNOWLEDGMENTS

Thank you to my husband, Justin, for your endless support, pep talks, and for believing in me. Thank you for encouraging me throughout this process and for being so proud of my work. Your belief in me gave me the confidence to write this book. Thank you for your patience, love, and constant praise. You always know just what to say.

Thank you to my two precious sons, Jacob and Joshua. You are both my "why." Through writing this book, I hope to be an example of a hard-working mother who wants what is best for her children. Everything I do is for you both! I love you with my heart and soul.

Thank you to my parents. Mom, your passion, dedication, and love for teaching inspires me every day. Thank you for going through my book with me, for being one of my biggest supporters, and for always being a voice of reason and positivity. You are a model mother and educator, and when I grow up I want to be like you. And to my dad, Ernie. Thank you for always showing me the value of hard work and for modeling what it's like to put your family first. You've always shown how proud you are of what I've accomplished and your belief in me makes me stronger. Thank you both for loving me unconditionally and for supporting me through this process.

Thank you to my sister, Marisa. You may be younger than me, but you always have the best advice. Thank you for supporting me through this process and for giving me unfiltered and real feedback. Thank you for being there for me every day. I am grateful you are my sister.

Thank you to my former student teacher and forever friend, Annie. While we worked together when you were student teaching you reminded me why I started teaching in the first place. Your enthusiasm and love for teaching inspired me to be better for my students. In addition to being a teaching inspiration, you've also become one of my closest friends. Thank you for being a listening ear and for supporting me through the ups and downs.

Thank you to one of my most supportive grade-level teammates and forever friend, Adina. Working with you showed me that teacher clarity and collective teacher efficacy really does work! You are a wonderful educator and your belief in me made me a better teacher. Thank you for your encouragement and for being such a wonderful friend.

Thank you to two of my most influential principals, Carin and Sandy. Without your support, guidance, and belief in me and my teaching abilities I would not be the teacher I am today. Your knowledge, passion, and intentionality in leading has inspired me more than you both know. I am grateful for your mentorship, friendship, and our coalition of intentional peers.

Thank you to Professor John Hattie and his many colleagues whose work has inspired and informed *Getting Started with Teacher Clarity*. Your research and analysis on effective teaching practices has transformed the way I teach, assess, and shape my classroom and students' learning experiences.

Thank you to my editor, Claire Sielaff, and the team at Ulysses Press. I am so thankful for your guidance, patience, and support throughout this process. Thank you for helping me create and distribute my first book about something I am so passionate about.

ABOUT THE AUTHOR

Marine Freibrun earned her bachelor of arts from the University of California, Irvine, and her master of arts in educational leadership from California State University, Northridge. She is currently a 5th-grade teacher who has previously taught 2nd, 3rd, 6th, and 8th grade. She has also served as an instructional coach, English Language Development coach, and Positive Behavior Interventions and Supports coach for her district, as well as the head teacher for her school site. Marine enjoys working with teachers through professional development and mentorship, all while continuously learning new, effective methods to implement in her daily teaching. She is also the author of the blog *Tales from a Very Busy Teacher*. She lives in southern Idaho with her two amazing boys and supportive husband.